Jesintha

Sustainable Home Renovation: Eco-Friendly Remodeling for a Greener Future

Practical Guide to Energy-Efficient Upgrades and Green Living

Praise the Lord

Copyright © 2025 by Jesintha Bhaskaran

All rights reserved. No part of this publication may be reproduced, stored or transmitted in any form or by any means, electronic, mechanical, photocopying, recording, scanning, or otherwise without written permission from the publisher. It is illegal to copy this book, post it to a website, or distribute it by any other means without permission.

Jesintha Bhaskaran has no responsibility for the persistence or accuracy of URLs for external or third-party Internet Websites referred to in this publication and does not guarantee that any content on such Websites is, or will remain, accurate or appropriate.

First edition

Introduction: Welcome to a Greener Home 5

Chapter 1: Where Do I Even Start? (The Planning Phase) 10

Chapter 2: Energy Efficiency - The Secret to Lower Bills 23

Chapter 3: Water Conservation - Every Drop Counts 40

Chapter 4: Sustainable Materials - Build Smart, Build Green 62

Chapter 5: Reducing Waste During Renovation 81

Chapter 6: Smart Home, Sustainable Home 100

Chapter 7: Indoor Air Quality - Breathing Cleaner at Home 125

Chapter 8: Sustainable Kitchens and Bathrooms 150

Chapter 9: The Outdoor Space - Making Your Yard Eco-Friendly 175

Chapter 10: Living the Green Lifestyle After the Renovation 202

Conclusion: Your Home, Your Impact 229

About the Author 235

Introduction: Welcome to a Greener Home

The Moment That Changed Everything

I still remember the exact moment my perspective on home renovation changed forever. It wasn't during some grand environmental conference or after reading an article on climate change. It was something much simpler, something closer to home.

It was a scorching summer afternoon, and my electricity bill had just arrived. As I ripped open the envelope, my eyes widened. It was nearly double what I had expected. The air conditioning had been running non-stop, my old refrigerator hummed loudly in the background, and the lights were always on, even when no one was in the room. But what really struck me wasn't just the money I was wasting—it was the realization that my home, the place I loved and cherished, was incredibly inefficient.

I started asking questions: *Why was my house consuming so much energy? Could I do something about it? Would it cost me a fortune to fix?* That's when I began my journey into sustainable home renovation. And now, I want to take you along on this journey too.

Why Sustainable Renovation Matters (For Your Home, Wallet, and the Planet)

Many people assume that home renovation is purely about aesthetics—new countertops, a fresh coat of paint, maybe some stylish flooring. But the reality is that renovation is also about efficiency, sustainability, and long-term value. Here's why making your home greener isn't just a "nice idea" but a necessary step for the future:

1. It Saves You Money (A Lot of It!)

Let's be honest—one of the biggest concerns with home improvement is the cost. No one wants to spend more money than necessary, and sustainable upgrades often seem expensive at first glance. But here's the truth: sustainable choices are actually more cost-effective in the long run.

- Energy-efficient appliances lower your electricity bills.
- Proper insulation reduces heating and cooling costs.
- Water-saving fixtures cut down on your water bill.
- Durable, eco-friendly materials last longer, saving you money on replacements.

Would you rather pay a slightly higher upfront cost and save thousands in the long run, or keep paying sky-high utility bills month after month? That's a no-brainer, right?

2. It Makes Your Home Healthier

Did you know that many traditional paints, carpets, and construction materials release toxic chemicals into the air? These volatile organic compounds (VOCs) can cause headaches, allergies, and long-term health issues. A green home uses non-toxic materials that improve air quality, making it a healthier space for you and your family.

3. It Boosts Your Home's Value

The real estate market is evolving, and buyers are getting smarter. More and more people are looking for energy-efficient homes that promise lower utility bills and a smaller carbon footprint. Investing in sustainable renovations today means a higher resale value tomorrow.

4. It Helps the Planet (Without You Doing Anything Drastic)

You don't have to live off the grid or build a tiny house to make an impact. Small sustainable choices—like choosing LED lights, installing solar panels, or using recycled materials—reduce waste, lower carbon emissions, and help combat climate change. Imagine the impact if every homeowner made even a few of these changes!

Common Myths About Green Renovations (And Why They Aren't True)

When I first started researching sustainable renovation, I ran into so many misconceptions that almost scared me away. Maybe you've heard some of these too:

Myth #1: Sustainable Renovation Is Too Expensive

This is probably the biggest myth out there. Yes, some eco-friendly materials and energy-efficient systems can have a higher upfront cost, but the savings over time far outweigh the initial investment. Plus, government incentives and rebates can significantly reduce costs.

Myth #2: It's Only for New Homes

Wrong! Whether you live in a hundred-year-old house or a modern apartment, there are always ways to improve sustainability. From upgrading insulation to choosing better materials, every home can become more energy-efficient.

Myth #3: It's Too Complicated

You don't need to be an architect or environmental scientist to make green choices. Many upgrades—like switching to LED bulbs, sealing air leaks, or using low-flow faucets—are simple and easy to implement.

Myth #4: You Have to Sacrifice Style for Sustainability

Absolutely not! Sustainable design is as stylish as ever. Bamboo flooring, recycled glass countertops, and VOC-free paints come in a wide range of colors and styles. You can have a stunning home that's also eco-friendly.

How to Use This Book: Small Steps or Big Changes—Your Choice!

This book isn't about forcing you into a complete home overhaul. Instead, it's about giving you options. Whether you're planning a major renovation or just want to make a few changes, you'll find practical, easy-to-follow advice here.

- **If you're starting small:** You'll find simple, budget-friendly tips that you can implement today.
- **If you're planning a big remodel:** I'll guide you through sustainable materials, energy efficiency, and waste reduction.
- **If you're somewhere in between:** That's perfect too! Pick and choose what works for you.

The goal is progress, not perfection. Every small step makes a difference.

My Own Journey with Sustainability

I wasn't always someone who cared about eco-friendly choices. In fact, when I first bought my home, I was more focused on aesthetics than efficiency. But after that eye-opening moment with my sky-high electricity bill, I started making small changes.

- I switched out my old incandescent bulbs for LEDs.
- I installed a smart thermostat to better regulate my home's temperature.
- I started looking for second-hand furniture instead of buying new.
- I chose low-VOC paint when I repainted my walls.

And the best part? Not only did I save money, but my home felt fresher, cleaner, and more comfortable. Over time, these small choices turned into a passion. Now, I want to share everything I've learned so you can create a home that's not just beautiful, but sustainable too.

Let's Get Started!

Are you ready to transform your home into a greener, more energy-efficient space? Whether you want to reduce your utility bills, create a healthier home, or simply do your part for the planet, you're in the right place.

Let's dive in and explore the many ways you can make your home more sustainable—one step at a time.

Chapter 1: Where Do I Even Start? (The Planning Phase)

Section 1: Evaluating Your Home's Current Sustainability Score

So, you've decided to make your home more sustainable—great choice! But before you start picking out eco-friendly materials or researching solar panels, you need to take a step back and evaluate where your home currently stands. After all, you wouldn't start a road trip without knowing your starting point, right? The same principle applies here. To make meaningful changes, you need to understand your home's strengths and weaknesses in terms of sustainability.

Why Evaluating Your Home Matters

Many homeowners dive headfirst into renovations without properly assessing their home's current state. The result? They might end up spending money on upgrades that don't offer much impact while overlooking the real problem areas. Evaluating your home's sustainability score helps you:

- Identify the biggest energy wasters.
- Pinpoint cost-effective improvements.
- Prioritize what to tackle first based on impact and budget.
- Track progress as you implement changes.

Think of it like a doctor's check-up for your home. You wouldn't start treatment without a diagnosis, and in the same way, you shouldn't begin a renovation without a clear understanding of what needs improvement.

The Sustainability Score: What Are We Measuring?

When we talk about a home's sustainability, we're really looking at five key factors:

1. **Energy Efficiency** – How much electricity and gas does your home consume?
2. **Water Usage** – Are you using water efficiently, or is it literally going down the drain?
3. **Indoor Air Quality** – Are the materials in your home contributing to a healthy environment?
4. **Waste Management** – How much waste do you generate, and how much do you recycle?
5. **Material Sustainability** – Were your home's materials sourced ethically and sustainably?

Each of these areas plays a role in how "green" your home really is. Now, let's break them down one by one so you can get a clearer picture of where your home stands.

---

1. Energy Efficiency: Is Your Home an Energy Hog?

The first step is figuring out how much energy your home is using—and wasting. Take a look at your last few utility bills. Are your energy costs consistently high? Do they spike in summer or winter? These are signs of inefficiencies in heating, cooling, or insulation.

How to Check Your Home's Energy Efficiency:

- **The Touch Test:** Place your hand near windows and doors. If you feel a draft, you're losing valuable heating and cooling energy.

- **The Light Check:** Are you still using incandescent bulbs? LED bulbs use 75% less energy.
- **Appliance Audit:** Older refrigerators, washers, and HVAC systems can be energy hogs. Consider upgrading to ENERGY STAR-rated appliances.
- **Thermostat Efficiency:** Do you leave the thermostat running all day? A programmable or smart thermostat can cut energy waste significantly.
- **Insulation Inspection:** Poor insulation leads to high energy consumption. Check your attic, walls, and floors for gaps or thin insulation.

A home energy audit (either DIY or professional) can provide deeper insights into where you're losing energy. The good news? Fixing these issues can save you hundreds—if not thousands—of dollars over time.

---

2. Water Usage: Are You Using More Than You Need?

Many people don't think about water waste, but it's a big part of sustainability. If you've ever seen your water bill and wondered where all that water is going, chances are you have leaks, inefficient fixtures, or wasteful habits.

How to Check Your Home's Water Efficiency:

- **Leak Test:** Check faucets, pipes, and toilets for drips. A single dripping faucet can waste over 3,000 gallons of water a year.
- **Showerhead and Faucet Efficiency:** Older fixtures use much more water than necessary. Look for WaterSense-labeled products that use less water without sacrificing performance.

- **Outdoor Usage:** If you have a garden, how are you watering it? Sprinklers running in the middle of the day waste more water due to evaporation.
- **Toilet Efficiency:** Older toilets use up to 6 gallons per flush, while modern, efficient models use only 1.28 gallons.

If your water bill is higher than expected, you may want to start with small, simple upgrades like installing aerators on faucets or switching to a low-flow showerhead.

---

3. Indoor Air Quality: Are You Breathing Clean Air?

Sustainability isn't just about saving energy—it's also about creating a healthier living space. Many homes contain indoor pollutants from paints, carpets, furniture, and even cleaning supplies.

How to Check Your Home's Air Quality:

- **The Paint Test:** If your walls were painted with conventional paints, they might be releasing volatile organic compounds (VOCs) into the air.
- **Carpet & Upholstery Check:** Older carpets and furniture may contain flame retardants and chemicals that contribute to poor air quality.
- **Ventilation Review:** Does your home get fresh air circulation, or does it always feel stuffy?
- **Air Filter Inspection:** When was the last time you changed your HVAC filter? A dirty filter can circulate dust and allergens throughout your home.

Improving air quality can be as simple as adding houseplants (which naturally purify the air), using non-toxic cleaning products, and ensuring proper ventilation.

4. Waste Management: How Much Are You Throwing Away?

Sustainability also includes reducing waste. Take a look at your trash—how much of it is recyclable? How much is food waste? Many households throw away perfectly compostable or recyclable items simply because they don't have a system in place.

How to Evaluate Your Waste Habits:

- **Trash Audit:** For one week, track how much of your waste is actually recyclable or compostable.
- **Recycling Setup:** Do you have an easy system for separating recyclables?
- **Food Waste Check:** Are you throwing out a lot of unused food? Meal planning and composting can make a huge difference.
- **Reusable Products:** How many single-use plastics do you go through each week? Swapping to reusable bags, bottles, and containers can cut down waste significantly.

5. Material Sustainability: What's Your Home Made Of?

A truly sustainable home isn't just about efficiency—it's also about what materials were used to build and furnish it.

Key Questions to Ask:

- **Flooring:** Is your flooring made from sustainable materials like bamboo, reclaimed wood, or recycled tile?
- **Cabinetry & Furniture:** Were your cabinets made from solid wood or particleboard with toxic glues?
- **Countertops:** Are your countertops made from recycled materials, or are they energy-intensive materials like quartz and granite?
- **Paint & Finishes:** Did you use low-VOC or VOC-free paint?

Wrapping Up: Your Home's Sustainability Score

Now that you've evaluated your home, where do you stand? Maybe you've found that your energy use is high, but your waste management is already great. Or perhaps your air quality needs improvement, but your water usage is under control.

The point of this exercise isn't to feel overwhelmed—it's to create a starting point. Now that you know where your home needs improvement, you can start making a plan to tackle the biggest problem areas first.

Section 2: Setting Realistic Goals: Full Remodel vs. Small Upgrades

Once you have a clear picture of your home's sustainability score, it's time to set realistic goals. Should you go for a full remodel, or would small, strategic upgrades make a bigger impact? The answer depends on your budget, lifestyle, and long-term vision.

The Case for Small, Impactful Upgrades

Not everyone has the time or budget for a full-scale renovation, and that's okay. Small, incremental changes can have a surprisingly big impact. Here's how:

- **Energy Efficiency:** Replacing old bulbs with LEDs, adding weather stripping, and using smart thermostats.
- **Water Conservation:** Switching to low-flow fixtures and fixing leaks.
- **Air Quality:** Using non-toxic cleaners and adding houseplants.
- **Waste Reduction:** Implementing a recycling and composting system.

Each of these changes is budget-friendly and can be done in a day or weekend. They also provide immediate benefits without requiring a major investment.

The Full Remodel Approach

On the other hand, if you're planning a major home renovation, it's the perfect opportunity to integrate sustainability from the ground up. This could include:

- **Upgrading insulation and windows for better energy efficiency.**
- **Installing solar panels to reduce reliance on fossil fuels.**
- **Choosing sustainable building materials like reclaimed wood and recycled metal.**
- **Designing a water-efficient landscape with native plants and rainwater harvesting.**

While a full remodel requires a bigger budget, it can pay off in long-term energy savings and increased home value.

Finding the Right Balance

The key is to find the right balance between your goals and your resources. If you're not ready for a full remodel, focus on smaller, high-impact changes first. The great thing about sustainability is that every step—no matter how small—brings you closer to a greener, healthier home.

Section 3: Budgeting for Sustainability (and How It Saves Money Long-Term)

Now that you know what you want to achieve, it's time to talk about something that makes most homeowners nervous—money. The good news? A sustainable home doesn't have to break the bank. In fact, investing in sustainability can save you thousands of dollars over time.

The Myth That Green Homes Are Expensive

One of the biggest misconceptions about sustainable renovation is that it's too costly for the average homeowner. Sure, some upgrades—like solar panels—come with a higher upfront cost, but the long-term savings often outweigh the initial investment. Plus, many small, budget-friendly changes can have an immediate impact on both your utility bills and your home's sustainability.

Breaking Down the Costs

Here's a look at some common sustainable upgrades and how they pay off in the long run:

- **LED Light Bulbs** – Cost: $2-$5 per bulb; Savings: Up to $75 per year on electricity.
- **Smart Thermostat** – Cost: $100-$250; Savings: Around 10-15% on heating and cooling bills.
- **Low-Flow Showerheads** – Cost: $20-$50; Savings: Up to $100 per year on water and energy costs.
- **Weather Stripping & Insulation** – Cost: $100-$500; Savings: Hundreds of dollars per year in heating and cooling.
- **Solar Panels** – Cost: $10,000-$20,000; Savings: Up to $1,500 per year in electricity costs (plus tax credits).

While some of these upgrades require an upfront investment, they all pay for themselves over time. And the best part? Many states and local governments offer incentives, tax breaks, and rebates for making eco-friendly improvements.

Prioritizing Based on Budget

If you have a limited budget, start with the low-cost, high-impact changes first. Focus on areas where you'll see the most immediate return, such as:

- Sealing air leaks and adding insulation.
- Replacing inefficient lighting.
- Installing smart thermostats.
- Using water-saving fixtures.

As your budget allows, you can then work your way up to larger investments like solar panels and energy-efficient appliances.

The Long-Term Payoff

At the end of the day, sustainability isn't just about being eco-friendly—it's about creating a home that works smarter, not harder. The more efficient your home becomes, the less money you'll spend on wasted energy and resources. So, while the upfront costs may seem daunting, the long-term savings make it all worthwhile.

Section 4: Choosing Materials: What Makes Something Eco-Friendly?

When it comes to sustainable home renovation, one of the most important choices you'll make is selecting eco-friendly materials. But what exactly makes a material "green"?

The Three Key Factors of Sustainable Materials

1. **Renewability** – Is the material sourced from a renewable resource that can be replenished quickly?
2. **Recyclability & Reusability** – Can it be recycled or repurposed at the end of its life?
3. **Low Environmental Impact** – Does its production process minimize pollution and carbon emissions?

Examples of Sustainable Materials

- **Bamboo** – A rapidly renewable resource, bamboo is strong, durable, and perfect for flooring, cabinets, and furniture.
- **Reclaimed Wood** – Instead of cutting down new trees, reclaimed wood repurposes old timber for new uses.
- **Recycled Metal** – Aluminum and steel can be repurposed, reducing mining and production impacts.
- **Cork** – Harvested from the bark of cork trees without harming the tree itself, cork is a great choice for flooring and insulation.
- **Recycled Glass** – Used in countertops and tiles, it reduces landfill waste and has a stylish look.

- **Hempcrete** – A biocomposite made of hemp fibers and lime, offering excellent insulation properties.
- **Clay Plaster** – A natural alternative to synthetic drywall finishes, it improves indoor air quality and is biodegradable.

What to Avoid

- **Plastic-Based Materials** – They contribute to pollution and take centuries to break down.
- **Toxic Paints & Finishes** – Choose low-VOC (volatile organic compound) or VOC-free options.
- **Non-Sustainable Hardwoods** – Avoid woods like mahogany or teak unless certified by the FSC (Forest Stewardship Council).

By selecting materials that are durable, responsibly sourced, and recyclable, you'll reduce your home's environmental footprint while creating a healthier living space.

Section 5: Working with Contractors: Finding Green-Minded Professionals

Finding the right contractor can make or break your sustainable home renovation project. A contractor who understands and values sustainability will help ensure that your renovation aligns with your eco-friendly goals.

How to Identify Green-Minded Contractors

1. **Ask About Their Experience with Green Projects** – Not all contractors are familiar with sustainable building practices. Ask for examples of past projects that incorporated eco-friendly materials and energy-efficient designs.

2. **Look for Green Certifications** – Contractors who have certifications from organizations like LEED (Leadership in Energy and Environmental Design) or Green Building Initiative have demonstrated a commitment to sustainable building practices.
3. **Check Their Material Sourcing** – A truly green contractor will prioritize materials that are renewable, recycled, and non-toxic.
4. **Ask About Waste Management** – How do they handle construction waste? Do they recycle materials or send everything to a landfill?
5. **Look for Transparency in Pricing and Materials** – A contractor who is open about their sources and practices is more likely to align with your sustainability goals.
6. **Read Reviews and Ask for References** – Homeowners who have worked with green contractors can provide insights into their reliability and commitment to sustainability.

The Contractor Interview Process

Once you have a list of potential contractors, conduct interviews to ensure they're the right fit. Ask:

- What sustainable materials do you recommend?
- Do you have experience with energy-efficient home designs?
- How do you handle waste on your projects?
- Are you willing to work with recycled and reclaimed materials?

A good contractor should be enthusiastic about your sustainability goals and offer practical solutions to achieve them.

Summary of Chapter 1

- **Evaluating Your Home's Sustainability Score:** Understanding your home's strengths and weaknesses is the first step.
- **Setting Realistic Goals:** Whether you opt for small upgrades or a full remodel, planning your approach is key.
- **Budgeting Wisely:** Sustainable upgrades may have an upfront cost, but they pay off in the long run.
- **Choosing Materials:** Eco-friendly materials should be renewable, recyclable, and non-toxic.
- **Finding the Right Contractor:** A green-minded professional will help bring your vision to life.

By following these steps, you'll be well on your way to a more sustainable home, one that benefits both you and the planet.

Chapter 2: Energy Efficiency - The Secret to Lower Bills

Section 1: Understanding Your Home's Energy Flow

Imagine you're trying to fill a bucket with water, but it has several holes. No matter how much water you pour in, most of it leaks out. This is exactly what happens in an inefficient home. Your heating and cooling systems work tirelessly, yet a significant amount of energy escapes through leaks, drafts, poor insulation, and outdated appliances. If you don't understand how energy moves through your home, you might be unknowingly throwing money out the window—literally.

Why Understanding Energy Flow is Key

Many homeowners assume that high energy bills are just part of life. But what if you could cut those bills dramatically while also making your home more comfortable? The first step is figuring out how energy flows through your house and where it's being wasted.

Energy efficiency isn't just about saving money; it's also about reducing your carbon footprint. The less energy your home consumes, the fewer fossil fuels are burned to generate electricity. That means fewer greenhouse gas emissions, which is a win for both your wallet and the planet.

Identifying the Biggest Energy Wasters

Every home has weak spots where energy loss occurs. The most common culprits include:

1. **Windows and Doors** – Poorly sealed windows and doors can let in drafts, making your heating or cooling system work overtime.
2. **Insufficient Insulation** – If your home isn't properly insulated, it can't retain heat in winter or keep cool air in during summer.
3. **Old HVAC Systems** – An outdated heating, ventilation, and air conditioning (HVAC) system consumes more energy than necessary.
4. **Leaky Ductwork** – Gaps and leaks in ductwork can reduce HVAC efficiency by up to 30%.
5. **Inefficient Lighting and Appliances** – Incandescent bulbs and old appliances consume more electricity than modern energy-efficient options.
6. **Phantom Energy Drain** – Electronics and appliances that are plugged in but not in use still consume small amounts of energy.

Each of these factors contributes to higher energy consumption, but the good news is that all of them can be addressed with the right solutions.

The Importance of a Home Energy Audit

The best way to assess your home's energy efficiency is through a home energy audit. You can either hire a professional auditor or conduct a basic DIY audit yourself. Here's how each approach works:

Professional Energy Audit

A certified auditor uses specialized tools like infrared cameras, blower doors, and thermographic scans to pinpoint problem areas in your home. They can provide a detailed report with recommendations tailored to your home's specific needs.

What to Expect from a Professional Audit:

- A room-by-room examination of energy use.
- Identification of air leaks and insulation issues.
- Analyzing past energy bills to spot inefficiencies.
- Recommendations for upgrades that will provide the best return on investment.

DIY Energy Audit

If you prefer a hands-on approach, a DIY audit can still reveal major inefficiencies. Here's a simple checklist to follow:

- **Check for Drafts** – Hold a lit candle near windows, doors, and electrical outlets. If the flame flickers, you have a draft that needs sealing.
- **Inspect Insulation** – Look in the attic, walls, and crawl spaces to see if insulation is adequate.
- **Test Your HVAC System** – If your heating or cooling system struggles to maintain a steady temperature, it may need maintenance or an upgrade.
- **Monitor Appliance Usage** – Unplug devices when not in use and switch to energy-efficient models where possible.

Whether you opt for a professional or DIY audit, the insights gained will help you make informed decisions on improving your home's energy efficiency.

The Role of Smart Technology in Energy Management

Thanks to modern technology, monitoring and managing energy use has never been easier. Smart home devices allow homeowners to track real-time energy consumption and make adjustments as needed. Here are a few game-changing tools:

- **Smart Thermostats** – Devices like Nest or Ecobee learn your habits and adjust temperatures automatically to save energy.
- **Energy Monitoring Systems** – These devices track energy consumption per appliance, helping you identify where you can cut back.
- **Smart Power Strips** – They detect when electronics are in standby mode and cut off power to prevent phantom energy drain.
- **Automated Lighting Systems** – Motion-sensor lights and programmable schedules ensure that lights aren't left on unnecessarily.

By integrating these technologies, you can take control of your home's energy flow and make data-driven decisions that lead to lower bills and a smaller environmental footprint.

Taking the First Steps Towards an Energy-Efficient Home

Understanding your home's energy flow is the foundation of making impactful changes. Once you've identified the biggest energy wasters and conducted an energy audit, you're ready to take action. The upcoming sections of this chapter will guide you through practical steps to optimize insulation, upgrade appliances, and adopt energy-efficient habits that will save you money and make your home more sustainable.

Section 2: Insulation and Windows - The Game Changers

If you could only make two upgrades to improve your home's energy efficiency, insulation and windows should be at the top of your list. These two factors determine how well your home retains heat in the winter and stays cool in the summer. Without proper insulation and energy-efficient windows, your heating and cooling systems work overtime, leading to unnecessarily high energy bills.

The Science Behind Insulation

Insulation acts as a thermal barrier, slowing down the transfer of heat between your home's interior and exterior. In winter, it prevents warm air from escaping, and in summer, it keeps hot air out. The effectiveness of insulation is measured by its R-value—the higher the R-value, the better it resists heat transfer.

Where to Insulate for Maximum Efficiency

1. **Attic** – Since heat rises, an under-insulated attic is one of the biggest sources of energy loss.
2. **Walls** – Properly insulated walls prevent heat exchange with the outside environment.
3. **Floors** – Especially important for homes with crawl spaces or basements.
4. **Ductwork** – Insulating ducts reduces heat loss as air moves through your home.

Choosing the right type of insulation—fiberglass, spray foam, or rigid foam—depends on your home's structure and climate.

Windows: Your Home's Biggest Weak Spot

Windows are often the weakest link in a home's energy efficiency. Poorly sealed or single-pane windows allow heat to escape in winter and let unwanted heat in during summer. The solution? Energy-efficient windows with double or triple glazing, low-emissivity (Low-E) coatings, and proper sealing.

Upgrading to Energy-Efficient Windows

- **Double or Triple Glazing** – Multiple panes of glass trap insulating gas layers to reduce heat transfer.
- **Low-E Coatings** – These coatings reflect heat while allowing light to pass through, improving insulation without sacrificing brightness.
- **Window Seals and Weatherstripping** – Prevent air leaks that increase heating and cooling costs.

By investing in better insulation and windows, you create a home that stays comfortable year-round while significantly cutting energy costs. These upgrades also increase your property's value and reduce your environmental impact—making them smart, long-term investments.

Section 3: Smart Thermostats and Energy-Efficient HVAC Systems

If you could install just one piece of technology in your home that would make an immediate difference in your energy usage and costs, it would likely be a smart thermostat. These little devices have revolutionized home energy management, allowing homeowners to control heating and cooling with precision and efficiency. But they're just the beginning. Your HVAC (Heating, Ventilation, and Air Conditioning) system plays a massive role in your home's overall energy efficiency, and making the right upgrades here can mean significant savings on your energy bills.

The Power of Smart Thermostats

A smart thermostat isn't just a fancy digital control panel; it's an intelligent device that learns your habits and adjusts your home's temperature accordingly. Unlike traditional thermostats, which require manual adjustments or simple programmable schedules, smart thermostats use sensors and algorithms to optimize your home's climate control.

Here's what makes them a game-changer:

1. **Learning Your Schedule:** Many smart thermostats, like the Nest or Ecobee, learn when you're home and when you're away. Over time, they adjust your heating and cooling schedule automatically to match your lifestyle.
2. **Remote Control:** Forgot to turn down the heat before leaving for vacation? No problem. Smart thermostats allow you to adjust settings from your smartphone, no matter where you are.
3. **Energy Reports:** These devices provide data on your energy usage, helping you identify patterns and opportunities to save money.
4. **Integration with Smart Home Systems:** Many smart thermostats can sync with smart assistants like Alexa, Google Home, and Apple HomeKit, giving you voice control over your home's climate.
5. **Adaptive Features:** Some models monitor weather forecasts and adjust heating or cooling accordingly. If a cold front is coming, the thermostat may prepare by making gradual changes instead of sudden energy spikes.

Energy-Efficient HVAC Systems: The Heart of a Comfortable Home

Your home's heating and cooling system is often the biggest energy consumer. If your HVAC system is outdated, you could be wasting a lot of money every month. Fortunately, upgrading to an energy-efficient system can cut your energy bills significantly while also reducing your carbon footprint.

Here's what you need to know:

1. **High-Efficiency Furnaces and Boilers:** Modern high-efficiency furnaces use less fuel to produce the same amount of heat. Look for models with an Annual Fuel Utilization Efficiency (AFUE) rating of 90% or higher.
2. **Heat Pumps:** These systems provide both heating and cooling by transferring heat rather than generating it. Air-source heat pumps and geothermal heat pumps are among the most efficient options available today.
3. **Ductless Mini-Splits:** If you're looking for a way to heat and cool individual rooms efficiently, ductless mini-split systems are an excellent choice. They eliminate the energy loss associated with ductwork and provide targeted temperature control.
4. **Variable-Speed Air Conditioners:** Unlike traditional AC units that operate at full blast or not at all, variable-speed units adjust their output to match demand, reducing energy waste and maintaining consistent comfort.
5. **Zoned HVAC Systems:** These systems allow you to control temperatures in different areas of your home separately. If you spend most of your time in just a few rooms, zoning prevents you from wasting energy heating or cooling unused spaces.

Making the Right Choice for Your Home

If your HVAC system is more than 10-15 years old, it's worth considering an upgrade. But even if a full replacement isn't in the budget, there are still ways to improve efficiency:

1. **Regular Maintenance:** Changing filters, cleaning ducts, and servicing your HVAC system regularly can keep it running efficiently.
2. **Proper Insulation:** A well-insulated home reduces the workload on your heating and cooling system, making it more effective.
3. **Sealing Duct Leaks:** If you have central heating or air conditioning, leaky ducts can waste a huge amount of energy. Sealing them can improve efficiency by up to 20%.
4. **Smart Thermostat Integration:** Even with an older HVAC system, installing a smart thermostat can optimize performance and save you money.

The Financial Benefits of Smart Climate Control

Switching to a smart thermostat and upgrading your HVAC system isn't just about reducing energy waste—it's also about long-term savings. According to the U.S. Department of Energy, homeowners can save about 10% per year on heating and cooling costs by simply adjusting their thermostat by 7-10 degrees for 8 hours a day. With smart thermostats automating this process, those savings become effortless.

Additionally, many utility companies offer rebates for installing energy-efficient HVAC systems and smart thermostats, further lowering the cost of upgrades.

Final Thoughts

Investing in smart climate control isn't just a win for your wallet—it's a win for comfort, convenience, and sustainability. Whether you start with a smart thermostat or go all in with a high-efficiency HVAC system, these upgrades will make a tangible difference in your home's energy footprint. In the next section, we'll explore another key component of energy efficiency: lighting and appliances—how small changes can lead to big savings.

Section 4: Switching to LED Lighting and Energy-Efficient Appliances

When it comes to cutting energy costs and living more sustainably, people often think of big-ticket upgrades like solar panels or high-efficiency HVAC systems. But sometimes, the simplest changes can make the biggest impact. Switching to LED lighting and energy-efficient appliances is one of the easiest ways to start reducing your energy footprint today.

The Bright Idea: LED Lighting

Lighting accounts for about 15% of the average home's electricity use. Traditional incandescent bulbs are incredibly inefficient, wasting 90% of their energy as heat rather than light. That's where LED (Light Emitting Diode) bulbs come in.

Here's why LED bulbs are the clear winner:

1. **Lower Energy Consumption:** LEDs use up to 75% less energy than incandescent bulbs. That means if you replace all the bulbs in your home with LEDs, you could see a noticeable drop in your electricity bill.

2. **Long Lifespan:** Traditional bulbs last about 1,000 hours, while LED bulbs can last 25,000 hours or more. That means fewer replacements and less waste.
3. **Cooler Operation:** Since LEDs don't generate as much heat as incandescent bulbs, they help keep your home cooler in the summer, reducing the need for extra air conditioning.
4. **More Color and Brightness Options:** Modern LED bulbs come in a variety of color temperatures, from warm yellowish tones to cool daylight hues. You can even get dimmable and smart LED bulbs that integrate with home automation systems.

Making the Switch to LEDs

If you haven't switched to LED lighting yet, here's how to do it efficiently:

- **Start with high-use areas:** Replace bulbs in rooms where lights are on the most, such as the kitchen, living room, and bathrooms.
- **Look for ENERGY STAR-certified LEDs:** These bulbs meet strict energy efficiency standards and often qualify for rebates.
- **Consider smart LED bulbs:** These can be controlled remotely, scheduled to turn on and off, and even change color.
- **Use motion sensors and timers:** In places like hallways and outdoor spaces, these can reduce unnecessary energy use.

Switching to LEDs may seem like a small step, but when done throughout your home, it adds up to significant energy savings.

Energy-Efficient Appliances: Small Changes, Big Savings

Home appliances, from refrigerators to washing machines, contribute heavily to your home's overall energy consumption. Older appliances tend to be energy hogs, while modern energy-efficient models are designed to do the same job using less power.

Understanding ENERGY STAR Ratings

When shopping for new appliances, look for the **ENERGY STAR label**. This certification, issued by the U.S. Environmental Protection Agency, means that an appliance meets strict efficiency standards.

Here's what you need to know about energy-efficient appliances:

1. **Refrigerators:** Newer models use about 40% less energy than those made 15 years ago. If your fridge is over a decade old, it's probably costing you more than necessary.
2. **Washing Machines:** Front-loading washers use less water and require less energy to heat the water. They also remove more water during the spin cycle, reducing drying time.
3. **Dryers:** Energy-efficient dryers use moisture sensors to stop drying when clothes are done, preventing unnecessary energy use.
4. **Dishwashers:** Newer models use less water and heat more efficiently, helping to cut down on energy bills.
5. **Ovens and Stoves:** Induction cooktops are incredibly efficient, using electromagnetic energy to directly heat cookware without wasting energy on heating the surrounding air.

How to Upgrade to Energy-Efficient Appliances

If replacing appliances isn't in the budget right now, don't worry—there are still ways to reduce their energy consumption:

- **Unplug appliances when not in use:** Many electronics and kitchen gadgets draw power even when turned off. Plugging them into a power strip and switching it off can eliminate this "phantom" energy use.
- **Use cold water for laundry:** Heating water accounts for about 90% of the energy used by washing machines.
- **Only run full loads:** Whether it's the dishwasher or the washing machine, full loads make the most of the energy used.
- **Air-dry when possible:** Instead of using the dryer for every load, hang clothes to dry when the weather allows.
- **Keep fridge and freezer seals tight:** If you can slide a piece of paper between the door and seal, cold air is escaping, and your fridge is working harder than it should.

The Financial Benefits of Energy-Efficient Lighting and Appliances

While LED bulbs and efficient appliances may cost more upfront, they more than pay for themselves over time. Here's how:

- **LED bulbs last longer and use less energy, saving you money on electricity and replacement costs.**

- ENERGY STAR-certified appliances use up to 50% less energy, reducing your utility bills significantly over their lifespan.
- Many utility companies offer rebates for switching to energy-efficient appliances, further lowering the cost.

Final Thoughts

Switching to LED lighting and upgrading to energy-efficient appliances are two of the easiest and most effective ways to reduce your home's energy consumption. They require little effort, yet they yield significant savings and environmental benefits. In the next section, we'll explore another crucial step in maximizing energy efficiency—solar power and renewable energy options for your home.

Section 5: Solar Panels - Are They Worth It for You?

As we've explored different ways to improve your home's energy efficiency, one question naturally arises: Should you invest in solar panels? For many homeowners, solar energy represents the ultimate step toward sustainability and energy independence. But are solar panels right for you? Let's break it down.

How Do Solar Panels Work?

Solar panels convert sunlight into electricity using photovoltaic (PV) cells. These cells absorb sunlight and generate direct current (DC) electricity, which is then converted into alternating current (AC) power that your home can use. Excess energy can be stored in batteries or sent back to the grid, depending on your setup.

The Benefits of Solar Energy

1. **Lower Energy Bills:** Once installed, solar panels can significantly reduce or even eliminate your electricity bill. Some homeowners generate enough power to sell energy back to their utility company.
2. **Environmental Impact:** Solar energy is a clean, renewable power source that reduces your carbon footprint. By switching to solar, you help decrease dependence on fossil fuels.
3. **Energy Independence:** With solar panels and battery storage, you can protect yourself from power outages and rising electricity costs.
4. **Incentives and Tax Credits:** Many governments and utility companies offer rebates, tax credits, and incentives for homeowners who install solar panels, making them more affordable.

The Challenges of Going Solar

1. **High Upfront Costs:** Solar panel installation can be expensive, with costs varying based on system size and location. However, financing options and incentives can help offset this expense.
2. **Roof Suitability:** Not all roofs are ideal for solar panels. Factors such as shading from trees or buildings, roof angle, and structural integrity can affect performance.
3. **Maintenance and Repairs:** While solar panels require minimal maintenance, they may need occasional cleaning and repairs over their 25+ year lifespan.
4. **Weather Dependence:** Solar panels are most effective in sunny climates. If you live in an area with frequent cloudy days or long winters, your energy production may fluctuate.

Are Solar Panels Right for You?

To determine if solar panels are a good fit, consider the following:

- **Your Energy Consumption:** If your electricity bills are high, solar panels could provide significant savings.
- **Available Incentives:** Research local rebates and tax credits to reduce installation costs.
- **Sunlight Exposure:** Homes with plenty of direct sunlight will benefit the most from solar power.
- **Long-Term Plans:** Since solar panels have a long lifespan, they're best for homeowners planning to stay in their homes for many years.

Maximizing Your Solar Investment

If you decide to go solar, here are some tips to get the most out of your investment:

- **Work with a reputable installer:** Ensure your solar panels are properly installed for optimal efficiency.
- **Consider battery storage:** A solar battery can store excess energy for use during peak hours or power outages.
- **Monitor your system:** Many solar providers offer apps or monitoring systems to track energy production and usage.
- **Keep panels clean:** Dirt and debris can reduce efficiency, so periodic cleaning may be necessary.

Chapter 2 Summary

Energy efficiency is about making smart, sustainable choices that reduce your home's power consumption. We started by understanding where energy is lost and explored key upgrades like insulation, energy-efficient appliances, and smart thermostats. Switching to LED lighting and upgrading home appliances can significantly cut costs, while solar panels offer a long-term investment for homeowners looking to generate their own clean energy.

By making these changes, you're not just saving money—you're also taking an important step toward a greener, more self-sufficient home. As we move forward, we'll explore ways to improve water efficiency and reduce waste in your home. Sustainability isn't just about energy—it's about creating a healthier, more responsible lifestyle for you and future generations.

Chapter 3: Water Conservation - Every Drop Counts

Section 1: Detecting and Fixing Hidden Leaks

Water is one of the most precious resources we have, yet we often take it for granted. While we may be mindful of turning off the tap while brushing our teeth or using water-efficient appliances, hidden leaks can still waste hundreds or even thousands of gallons of water each year. If you've ever received an unexpectedly high water bill and wondered where all that water went, chances are, there's a leak somewhere in your home.

Why Hidden Leaks Matter

Leaks aren't just an inconvenience—they can cause serious problems over time. Wasted water means higher utility bills, potential damage to your home's structure, and even mold growth that can affect your indoor air quality. According to the Environmental Protection Agency (EPA), an average household leak can waste nearly 10,000 gallons of water per year. Fixing leaks is one of the easiest and most impactful steps you can take toward a more sustainable home.

How to Detect Hidden Leaks

Some leaks are obvious, like a dripping faucet or a running toilet, but others are more difficult to detect. Here are some practical ways to uncover hidden leaks in your home:

1. **Monitor Your Water Bill**
    - If your water usage spikes unexpectedly, it may indicate a leak.
    - Compare your monthly usage to previous months and look for patterns.

- If your water bill is consistently higher than usual without any change in household water habits, investigate further.

2. **Check Your Water Meter**
    - Locate your home's water meter (usually found outside near the curb or in a basement).
    - Turn off all water sources inside and outside your home.
    - Observe the meter—if it continues to move even when no water is being used, you likely have a leak.
    - Some meters have a small dial (often shaped like a triangle or wheel) that spins when water is flowing. If it moves while all taps are off, it's time to start searching for the culprit.

3. **Use the Food Coloring Test for Toilets**
    - Toilets are one of the most common sources of hidden leaks.
    - Add a few drops of food coloring to the toilet tank and wait 10-15 minutes.
    - If the color appears in the bowl without flushing, you have a leak in the flapper valve that needs to be fixed.

4. **Inspect Under Sinks and Around Appliances**
    - Check under kitchen and bathroom sinks for signs of moisture, mold, or water stains.
    - Look behind and under appliances like dishwashers, washing machines, and refrigerators with water dispensers.
    - If you notice warped cabinets, peeling paint, or a musty smell, water might be seeping where it shouldn't.

5. **Listen for Unusual Sounds**

- A faint hissing or dripping sound when no water is running could indicate a leak inside the walls or under the floors.
- Pay attention to changes in water pressure, as a sudden drop could signal a leak in the pipes.

Fixing Common Leaks

Once you've identified a leak, it's time to fix it. Many leaks are easy to repair without professional help, saving you money and preventing further water waste.

1. **Fixing Leaky Faucets**
   - The most common cause is a worn-out washer or cartridge inside the faucet handle.
   - Turn off the water supply, disassemble the faucet, replace the washer, and reassemble.
   - If you have a modern single-handle faucet, you may need to replace the entire cartridge.
2. **Repairing a Running Toilet**
   - Most running toilets are caused by a faulty flapper or fill valve.
   - Replace the flapper if it's warped or not sealing properly.
   - Adjust the float to ensure the correct water level in the tank.
3. **Patching Small Pipe Leaks**
   - For minor leaks in exposed pipes, use plumber's tape or epoxy putty as a temporary fix.
   - For a more permanent solution, cut out the damaged section of the pipe and replace it with a new piece using compression fittings.
4. **Sealing Leaks in Appliances**

- If your dishwasher or washing machine has a leak, check the hoses for cracks or loose connections.
- Replace worn-out hoses and tighten any loose fittings.
- Regularly clean the filters and check for signs of wear.

When to Call a Professional

While many leaks are easy to fix, some require professional help. If you suspect a leak inside your walls, under your foundation, or in your main water line, it's best to contact a plumber. Signs that you need expert assistance include:

- Water stains on ceilings or walls with no obvious source.
- A sudden drop in water pressure throughout your home.
- Unexplained puddles in the yard, indicating a possible underground leak.
- A persistent musty odor that suggests mold growth due to hidden moisture.

Preventing Future Leaks

The best way to deal with leaks is to prevent them from happening in the first place. Here are some proactive measures you can take:

- **Inspect pipes and appliances regularly** to catch small issues before they become major problems.
- **Install leak detectors** that sound an alarm or send alerts to your phone if they detect moisture.
- **Replace old plumbing fixtures** with newer, more durable models.

- **Avoid chemical drain cleaners** that can corrode pipes over time and lead to leaks.

The Impact of Fixing Leaks

By taking the time to detect and fix leaks, you're not only saving money but also contributing to water conservation efforts. A single dripping faucet can waste over 3,000 gallons of water per year—that's enough to fill more than 40 bathtubs! By making these small changes, you're taking an important step toward a more sustainable home.

As we continue this chapter, we'll explore other effective ways to conserve water, from upgrading to water-efficient fixtures to implementing smart landscaping techniques. Every drop counts, and with a few simple adjustments, you can make a big difference.

Section 2: Low-Flow Faucets, Showerheads, and Toilets

When people think of water conservation, they often imagine cutting back on usage—taking shorter showers, turning off the tap while brushing their teeth, or washing dishes more efficiently. While these habits are important, the real game-changer lies in upgrading to low-flow plumbing fixtures. Modern technology has made it possible to significantly reduce water consumption without sacrificing comfort or performance. In this section, we'll explore how low-flow faucets, showerheads, and toilets work, why they matter, and how to choose the best options for your home.

Why Low-Flow Fixtures Matter

Conserving water isn't just about reducing utility bills; it's about protecting one of Earth's most valuable resources. The average household in the U.S. uses around 300 gallons of water per day, and a significant portion of this is wasted through inefficient plumbing. Low-flow fixtures can cut water usage by 30% or more, making a noticeable difference in both environmental impact and household expenses.

Beyond personal savings, widespread adoption of water-efficient fixtures helps reduce the strain on local water supplies, especially in drought-prone areas. Cities and municipalities often offer rebates for upgrading to low-flow fixtures, making them an even more appealing investment.

Understanding Low-Flow Faucets

Traditional faucets release water at a rate of 2.2 gallons per minute (GPM) or more. In contrast, low-flow faucets deliver water at 1.5 GPM or lower, using aerators or laminar flow technology to maintain strong water pressure while reducing consumption.

How Low-Flow Faucets Work

- **Aerators**: These tiny attachments break up the water stream, mixing it with air to maintain pressure while using less water.
- **Laminar Flow**: Instead of aerating the water, some faucets use laminar flow, which delivers a steady, smooth stream without excess water waste.
- **Sensor and Touchless Faucets**: Many modern low-flow faucets come with motion sensors, automatically turning off the water when not in use, preventing unnecessary waste.

Choosing the Right Low-Flow Faucet

When shopping for a low-flow faucet, look for the **WaterSense** label, a certification from the U.S. Environmental

Protection Agency (EPA) ensuring efficiency and performance. Consider additional features like temperature control, touchless operation, and ease of installation.

The Power of Low-Flow Showerheads

Few things are more refreshing than a nice, strong shower. However, traditional showerheads use **2.5 GPM or more**, meaning a 10-minute shower can consume **25 gallons of water**. Low-flow showerheads bring this down to **1.5 GPM or even lower**, saving thousands of gallons per year without sacrificing comfort.

How Do Low-Flow Showerheads Maintain Comfort?

- **Aerated Showerheads**: Mix air with water, creating a misty, high-pressure effect while using less water.
- **Laminar-Flow Showerheads**: Deliver strong, individual water streams, maintaining heat better than aerated versions.
- **Pulsating or Multi-Setting Showerheads**: Offer different spray patterns, allowing you to choose the most comfortable flow.

Selecting the Best Low-Flow Showerhead

Just like faucets, look for the **WaterSense** label to ensure efficiency. Additionally, consider models with adjustable settings so you can control spray strength and coverage. Some showerheads also feature **pause buttons**, letting you temporarily stop water flow while soaping up, further reducing usage.

The Impact of Low-Flow Toilets

Toilets account for **nearly 30% of household water use**, making them one of the best places to implement water-saving technology. Older toilets use **3.5 to 7 gallons per flush (GPF)**, whereas modern low-flow models use **1.28 GPF or less**, significantly reducing water waste.

Types of Low-Flow Toilets

- **Gravity-Flush Toilets**: Use the natural force of gravity to move waste with minimal water.
- **Pressure-Assisted Toilets**: Utilize air pressure to create a strong, efficient flush while using less water.
- **Dual-Flush Toilets**: Provide two flushing options—one for liquid waste (0.8 GPF) and one for solid waste (1.28 GPF), offering customizable water savings.

Choosing the Right Low-Flow Toilet

When upgrading, check for the **WaterSense** certification to ensure efficiency. Look for features like **comfort height**, **elongated bowls** for added comfort, and **efficient flushing technology** to prevent clogs while maintaining water savings.

Installation and Costs

Upgrading to low-flow fixtures is easier than most people think. Many faucets and showerheads simply screw onto existing plumbing, requiring minimal tools and effort. Toilets may require professional installation, but the long-term savings make the investment worthwhile.

Conclusion: Small Changes, Big Impact

Switching to low-flow faucets, showerheads, and toilets is one of the simplest yet most effective ways to conserve water in your home. These small upgrades drastically reduce daily consumption, lower utility bills, and contribute to global water conservation efforts. By choosing the right fixtures and making the switch, you're not only improving your home's sustainability but also taking a meaningful step toward protecting our planet's most precious resource.

Section 3: Harvesting Rainwater for Gardening and Home Use

Why Harvest Rainwater?

Water is one of the most precious resources we have, and yet, much of it goes to waste. Every time it rains, gallons of water flow off our rooftops, driveways, and sidewalks, only to end up in storm drains. But what if we could capture that water and use it effectively? Rainwater harvesting is an age-old practice that has regained popularity as more homeowners look for sustainable ways to reduce their environmental footprint and lower utility bills.

Harvesting rainwater isn't just about saving money on your water bill—it's about self-sufficiency and making the most of natural resources. Whether you use the collected water for gardening, flushing toilets, or even for household cleaning, every drop you save contributes to a more sustainable lifestyle.

Understanding the Basics of Rainwater Harvesting

Rainwater harvesting is the process of collecting and storing rainwater for later use. It involves a simple system that captures runoff from your roof or other surfaces, filters it, and then stores it in a tank for future use. Depending on your needs, the system can be as basic as a rain barrel under a downspout or as advanced as an underground cistern with a filtration system for household water use.

The main components of a rainwater harvesting system include:

1. **Catchment Area** – Usually your rooftop, where rainwater first lands.
2. **Gutters and Downspouts** – Channels that direct the water from your roof to a collection system.
3. **Filtration System** – Removes debris and contaminants.
4. **Storage Tank or Barrel** – Holds the collected rainwater.
5. **Distribution System** – Pipes or hoses that direct the stored water where needed.

Each of these components plays a vital role in ensuring that the water you collect is clean and useful.

How to Set Up a Basic Rainwater Harvesting System

Getting started with rainwater harvesting doesn't require an engineering degree. Here's how you can set up a simple yet effective system at home:

1. **Choose a Collection Point**

The best place to collect rainwater is from your rooftop, as it provides a large surface area and is free from contaminants found at ground level. If your home has gutters, you're already halfway there. Make sure they are clean and free from debris so water can flow smoothly into your collection system.

2. Install a Rain Barrel or Storage Tank

For beginners, a rain barrel is a great place to start. These barrels can hold anywhere from 50 to 100 gallons of water and are easy to install under a downspout. If you need more water storage, consider a larger cistern that can be placed above or below ground.

Make sure your storage container has a secure lid to prevent mosquitoes and debris from entering. You may also want to install an overflow system to direct excess water away from your home's foundation.

3. Add a Filtration System

Rainwater may carry dirt, leaves, or small debris, so a simple filter is essential. You can place a mesh screen over the opening of your barrel or install a first-flush diverter, which redirects the first few gallons of rainwater away from your storage tank to remove contaminants.

4. Set Up a Distribution System

Once your rainwater is collected, you'll need a way to use it. Many people attach a hose to their rain barrel to water their garden, while more advanced setups use pumps and underground pipes to distribute water throughout the home for flushing toilets or doing laundry.

Uses of Harvested Rainwater

Once you have a functioning rainwater harvesting system, you can use the water in various ways:

- **Gardening and Landscaping:** One of the best uses for harvested rainwater is irrigating plants. Rainwater is free of the chemicals and minerals found in tap water, making it better for plants.
- **Flushing Toilets:** With a bit of plumbing work, you can connect your system to your toilets, reducing the amount of municipal water you use.
- **Laundry and Cleaning:** Non-potable rainwater can be used for household cleaning and even washing clothes.
- **Refilling Outdoor Water Features:** Ponds, fountains, and birdbaths can all be replenished with harvested rainwater.

Benefits of Rainwater Harvesting

1. Reduces Water Bills

One of the most immediate benefits of rainwater harvesting is a noticeable drop in your water bill. By using collected rainwater for non-drinking purposes, you decrease your dependence on municipal water.

2. Prevents Flooding and Soil Erosion

Excess rainwater can cause flooding and soil erosion, especially in areas with poor drainage. A rainwater harvesting system captures this water before it can create problems in your yard.

3. Provides a Backup Water Source

During droughts or water shortages, having a backup supply of rainwater can be incredibly beneficial. Even if you can't drink it without proper treatment, it can still serve many household purposes.

4. Supports Sustainable Living

Harvesting rainwater reduces your reliance on municipal water sources, conserves energy used in water treatment, and helps reduce the overall demand for freshwater supplies.

Overcoming Common Concerns

Some people hesitate to start rainwater harvesting due to common concerns. Let's address a few:

- **"Rainwater is dirty."** While rainwater may contain pollutants from the air or roof, simple filtration methods make it safe for most household uses.
- **"It won't rain enough to make a difference."** Even in areas with less rainfall, you'd be surprised how much water you can collect. A 1,000-square-foot roof can yield over 600 gallons of water from just one inch of rain!
- **"Setting up a system is too expensive."** While larger systems with pumps and underground tanks can be costly, a basic rain barrel system is affordable and offers immediate savings.

Final Thoughts

Harvesting rainwater is an easy, effective, and sustainable way to conserve water and reduce your environmental footprint. Whether you start small with a single rain barrel or go big with a whole-home system, every drop you save helps build a more sustainable future.

Section 4: Greywater Systems: Recycling Water Safely

The Case for Greywater Recycling

Water is a precious resource, and as homeowners, we often use far more than we need. While rainwater harvesting focuses on collecting fresh water, greywater recycling takes things a step further by reusing the water we've already used—water from sinks, showers, washing machines, and dishwashers. The idea of recycling used water might seem unusual at first, but with the right system in place, it's an effective way to conserve water without compromising hygiene or convenience.

Greywater systems have become increasingly popular among eco-conscious homeowners because they offer a simple yet effective way to reduce water waste. Instead of sending all used household water down the drain, a greywater system filters and redirects it for secondary purposes, such as irrigating your garden, flushing toilets, or even supplying a secondary water source for washing machines. This approach not only lowers water consumption but also decreases the burden on municipal wastewater systems, leading to a more sustainable home.

What Is Greywater, and What Isn't?

Before diving into how to install and use a greywater system, it's essential to understand the distinction between greywater and blackwater.

- **Greywater**: This is the relatively clean wastewater from your home that comes from showers, bathtubs, sinks, washing machines, and dishwashers. It contains small amounts of soap, grease, and dirt but is still safe for reuse with proper treatment.

- **Blackwater**: This is wastewater from toilets, kitchen sinks, and anything containing human waste or significant food scraps. Blackwater requires more extensive treatment and is not suitable for home greywater systems.

Understanding this difference ensures that you are recycling water safely without risking contamination or health hazards.

The Benefits of Greywater Systems

Installing a greywater system in your home comes with multiple advantages:

- **Reduces water consumption**: A greywater system can cut your home's water usage by up to 50%, lowering utility bills and reducing dependence on municipal water supplies.
- **Supports sustainable landscaping**: Many homeowners use greywater for irrigation, reducing the need for potable water to keep their gardens lush and healthy.
- **Lowers wastewater output**: By diverting water from drains, greywater systems reduce the volume of wastewater sent to treatment plants, lessening strain on local sewage infrastructure.
- **Saves money**: Beyond lowering water bills, greywater systems may qualify for tax incentives or rebates in certain areas, making them a financially smart investment.

Types of Greywater Systems

There are several greywater systems available, ranging from simple to advanced, depending on your needs and budget.

1. **Bucket System (Manual Collection)**
    - The simplest and least expensive method of greywater recycling.
    - Collects water manually from sinks or bathtubs using buckets and reuses it for watering plants.
    - While effective, this method requires effort and isn't ideal for large-scale water conservation.
2. **Diversion Systems (Basic Gravity-Fed Systems)**
    - Redirects greywater from washing machines, sinks, or showers to an outdoor irrigation system.
    - Typically involves a three-way valve that allows users to send water to the garden when needed.
    - Requires basic plumbing modifications but is relatively low-maintenance.
3. **Pump-Based Systems (Pressurized Delivery)**
    - Collects greywater in a holding tank and uses a small pump to distribute it for landscape irrigation or toilet flushing.
    - Offers more control over where the water is used and allows for storage.
    - Requires filters to remove debris and prevent clogs in pipes.
4. **Treatment-Based Systems (Advanced Filtration and Reuse)**
    - Includes filtration and disinfection processes, such as sand filters, UV light, or biofiltration.
    - Produces water clean enough for non-potable uses like laundry, toilet flushing, and garden irrigation.
    - More expensive and requires regular maintenance but provides the highest level of water reuse.

How to Install a Greywater System Safely

If you're ready to set up a greywater system in your home, here's how to do it correctly:

1. **Check Local Regulations**
   - Some cities and states have strict regulations regarding greywater use. Check with your local water authority to ensure compliance.
2. **Choose the Right System**
   - Decide whether you need a simple gravity-fed system, a pump-based system, or a fully treated system based on your household's water usage and goals.
3. **Use Biodegradable Soaps and Detergents**
   - Many household soaps contain phosphates and chemicals that can harm plants. Use biodegradable and non-toxic products to ensure the safety of your greywater system.
4. **Install Proper Filtration**
   - A basic filter can remove large particles and prevent clogs. Advanced systems may use UV treatment or biological filtration to improve water quality.
5. **Direct Water to the Right Areas**
   - Never use greywater for watering edible plants unless it has been treated. It's best suited for ornamental plants, trees, or flushing toilets.
6. **Maintain the System Regularly**
   - Clean filters and pipes periodically to prevent blockages and ensure smooth operation.

Potential Challenges and How to Overcome Them

While greywater systems are highly beneficial, they do come with challenges. Here's how to address common issues:

- **Soap and chemical buildup**: Stick to eco-friendly cleaning products to prevent harmful residues from affecting your plants.
- **Clogged pipes**: Install a mesh filter at the collection point and clean it regularly.
- **Unpleasant odors**: If your greywater system starts to smell, it may need better ventilation or a bacterial treatment to break down organic matter.
- **Regulatory hurdles**: If local laws restrict greywater use, consider advocacy efforts or working with professionals to meet code requirements.

The Future of Water Conservation at Home

Greywater systems represent a crucial step in making our homes more sustainable. As water shortages and environmental concerns grow, finding ways to reduce waste and recycle existing resources will become increasingly important. By adopting a greywater system, you're not just lowering your water bill—you're making a conscious choice to protect the environment and ensure a more sustainable future for the next generation.

Section 5: Sustainable Landscaping for a Water-Efficient Yard

When we think about saving water in our homes, we often focus on fixing leaks or installing efficient fixtures. But one of the biggest water guzzlers is sitting right outside our front door—the yard. Traditional landscaping, with its lush green lawns and water-hungry plants, can waste thousands of gallons of water each year. The good news? You don't have to sacrifice beauty to create a sustainable, water-efficient yard. By choosing the right plants, improving soil health, and rethinking how we use water outdoors, you can have a stunning garden that thrives with minimal water use.

Rethinking the Traditional Lawn

For many homeowners, a well-manicured green lawn is a symbol of pride. But maintaining that perfect grass patch comes at a steep cost—both financially and environmentally. Lawns require constant watering, fertilizers, and mowing, which contribute to excessive water consumption and pollution. If you live in a dry or drought-prone area, traditional lawns may not be sustainable at all.

So, what's the alternative? One option is to reduce the size of your lawn or eliminate it altogether. Many homeowners are switching to native ground covers, artificial turf, or gravel gardens that require little to no watering. If you love the look of grass, opt for drought-resistant grass varieties like buffalo grass or fescue, which require far less water than traditional Kentucky bluegrass.

Choosing Native and Drought-Tolerant Plants

The secret to a water-efficient yard lies in choosing the right plants. Native plants—those that naturally grow in your region—are already adapted to the local climate, meaning they need less water and maintenance. They also support local wildlife, providing food and shelter for birds, bees, and butterflies.

Drought-tolerant plants, such as succulents, lavender, and ornamental grasses, thrive with little water. These plants are not only practical but also add unique textures and colors to your landscape. You can create beautiful, diverse garden beds with a mix of flowering perennials, shrubs, and trees that can survive on rainfall alone.

A good rule of thumb is to group plants with similar water needs together. This technique, called hydrozoning, ensures that you're not overwatering drought-resistant plants while trying to keep thirstier plants alive.

Improving Soil Health for Better Water Retention

Healthy soil is the foundation of a water-efficient yard. Poor, compacted soil repels water, causing it to run off rather than soak in. This leads to wasted water and unhealthy plants. To improve soil health, focus on organic practices like adding compost, mulch, and organic matter.

Mulching is one of the simplest and most effective ways to conserve water in your garden. A layer of mulch around plants helps retain moisture, regulate soil temperature, and prevent weeds from competing for water. Organic mulches, such as wood chips, straw, or leaves, break down over time, enriching the soil and improving its ability to hold water.

Compost also plays a crucial role in sustainable landscaping. Mixing compost into your soil increases its ability to retain moisture and nutrients, reducing the need for frequent watering. Plus, composting yard waste and food scraps keeps organic material out of landfills and reduces greenhouse gas emissions.

Watering Wisely: Efficient Irrigation Methods

Even with the best drought-tolerant plants and soil practices, some watering will still be necessary. The key is to do it wisely. Traditional sprinkler systems are inefficient and often waste water through evaporation and runoff. Instead, consider these smart watering techniques:

- **Drip irrigation:** This system delivers water directly to the roots of plants, reducing evaporation and ensuring efficient water use.
- **Soaker hoses:** These hoses slowly release water into the soil, preventing runoff and minimizing waste.
- **Rainwater harvesting:** Collecting rainwater in barrels or underground cisterns provides a free and sustainable water source for your garden.
- **Watering at the right time:** Water early in the morning or late in the evening to prevent evaporation from the hot midday sun.

By making small changes to how and when you water, you can significantly reduce water waste while keeping your plants healthy.

Sustainable Hardscaping: Reducing Water-Intensive Features

Hardscaping—features like patios, walkways, and decorative rocks—can play a big role in water conservation. Instead of expansive lawns, consider incorporating permeable paving materials like gravel, porous concrete, or brick pavers, which allow water to seep into the ground instead of running off into storm drains.

Rock gardens, dry creek beds, and xeriscaping (landscaping designed for minimal water use) can add beauty and functionality to your outdoor space without the need for constant watering. You can also create designated rain gardens—planting areas that collect and absorb rainwater runoff, helping to prevent erosion and reduce flooding.

Summary: Creating a Water-Smart Landscape

A water-efficient yard is not only better for the environment but also saves you money on water bills and reduces maintenance. By choosing native and drought-tolerant plants, improving soil health, using efficient irrigation methods, and incorporating sustainable hardscaping, you can create a beautiful, thriving outdoor space that requires minimal water.

The shift to sustainable landscaping doesn't have to happen overnight. Start with small changes—replace a portion of your lawn with native plants, install a rain barrel, or add mulch to your garden beds. Every step you take makes a difference.

Water conservation is not just about using less—it's about using it wisely. With thoughtful planning, your yard can become a resilient, self-sustaining oasis that supports local ecosystems while reducing your household's environmental footprint.

Chapter 4: Sustainable Materials - Build Smart, Build Green

Section 1: What to Look for in Sustainable Wood, Tiles, and Countertops

When it comes to home renovations, materials matter—a lot. Every piece of wood, tile, or countertop you choose has an impact not just on your home's aesthetics and durability but also on the environment. The good news? Sustainable options abound. The challenge is knowing what to look for and how to make choices that align with your green renovation goals. Let's dive into the details so you can make informed, eco-friendly choices for your home.

Sustainable Wood: Choosing Responsibly-Sourced Lumber

Wood is one of the most commonly used materials in home construction and renovation. However, deforestation and irresponsible harvesting practices have wreaked havoc on forests, biodiversity, and even local communities. If you love the warmth and versatility of wood but want to ensure you're making a responsible choice, here's what to consider:

1. **Look for Certification Labels**
   The easiest way to ensure your wood is sourced sustainably is by checking for certification labels. Two of the most trusted ones are:
   - **FSC (Forest Stewardship Council)** – Ensures wood is harvested sustainably while supporting local communities and biodiversity.
   - **PEFC (Programme for the Endorsement of Forest Certification)** – Another credible certification promoting responsible forest management.

2. **Opt for Reclaimed Wood**
   Reclaimed wood is salvaged from old buildings, barns, or even sunken logs. It reduces the demand for new lumber, keeps materials out of landfills, and often has a rustic, unique character that adds charm to any space.
3. **Consider Engineered Wood with Low VOCs**
   If you're choosing engineered wood products like plywood or MDF, look for low-VOC (volatile organic compounds) options. Traditional adhesives used in these products can release harmful chemicals into your home, affecting indoor air quality.
4. **Choose Fast-Growing Wood Species**
   Instead of slow-growing hardwoods like mahogany or teak, consider alternatives such as bamboo, cork, or fast-growing plantation wood like rubberwood. These are more renewable and don't contribute to deforestation.

Eco-Friendly Tiles: Beauty with a Green Touch

Tiles are a fantastic choice for floors, walls, and backsplashes, but not all tiles are created equal in terms of sustainability. Here's what to look for when selecting eco-friendly tiles:

1. **Recycled Content**
   Many tile manufacturers produce ceramic and glass tiles made from post-consumer and post-industrial waste. These recycled tiles require less energy to produce and help keep waste out of landfills.
2. **Locally Sourced Tiles**
   Shipping heavy materials like tiles over long distances increases their carbon footprint. Whenever possible, choose tiles that are manufactured locally or regionally to reduce transportation emissions.

3. **Natural Stone with Ethical Sourcing**
   If you love the look of natural stone, opt for responsibly quarried stone. Check if the company follows ethical labor practices and employs environmentally responsible extraction methods.
4. **Energy-Efficient Manufacturing**
   Some tile manufacturers use kilns powered by renewable energy, making their production process far more eco-friendly. Research the brand's sustainability initiatives before making a purchase.

Green Countertops: A Blend of Durability and Sustainability

Countertops are a major feature in kitchens and bathrooms, but traditional options like granite and quartz aren't always the greenest choices. Here are some eco-friendly alternatives:

1. **Recycled Glass Countertops**
   Made from crushed glass embedded in resin or concrete, these countertops are stunning, highly durable, and reduce landfill waste.
2. **Bamboo and Butcher Block**
   If you love the warmth of wood countertops, bamboo and sustainably harvested butcher block are great choices. They're renewable and biodegradable, making them an excellent green alternative.
3. **Recycled Paper Composite**
   Surprisingly durable and sleek, recycled paper countertops are made from post-consumer paper combined with non-toxic resins. They're resistant to water, heat, and stains.
4. **Concrete with Eco-Friendly Additives**
   Standard concrete has a high carbon footprint, but newer versions incorporate recycled materials like fly ash or slag to reduce emissions. Plus, concrete is

incredibly long-lasting, reducing the need for replacements.
5. **Quartz with Low-Impact Extraction**
While quartz is not the most sustainable option, some manufacturers produce it using recycled materials and sustainable mining practices. If quartz is your preference, research brands that prioritize environmental responsibility.

Final Thoughts

Choosing sustainable materials for your home renovation doesn't mean compromising on style or durability. By selecting responsibly sourced wood, eco-friendly tiles, and green countertops, you're making choices that benefit both your home and the planet. Each decision you make contributes to a healthier environment, a lower carbon footprint, and a beautiful, lasting space. In the next section, we'll explore how to ensure your home renovation incorporates non-toxic and safe building materials for a healthier indoor space.

Section 2: Reclaimed vs. New Materials: Pros and Cons

When renovating sustainably, one of the biggest decisions homeowners face is whether to use reclaimed materials or invest in new but eco-friendly options. Each choice comes with its own set of benefits and challenges, depending on budget, availability, and project scope.

The Case for Reclaimed Materials

Reclaimed materials are salvaged from old buildings, construction sites, or discarded furniture, giving them a second life instead of ending up in landfills. Here's why they're a great choice:

Pros:

- **Eco-Friendly:** Reusing materials reduces waste, conserves resources, and cuts down on pollution from new production.
- **Character and Uniqueness:** Older materials often have a weathered, aged look that adds charm and depth to your home.
- **Durability:** Many reclaimed materials, such as old-growth wood, are more durable than newly harvested materials due to their density and tight grain structure.
- **Cost Savings (Sometimes):** If sourced locally or salvaged from your own home, reclaimed materials can be budget-friendly.

Cons:

- **Limited Availability:** Finding the right reclaimed materials can take time and effort.
- **Quality Variability:** Some materials may need refinishing or reinforcement before they can be reused.
- **Potential for Contaminants:** Older materials may contain lead paint, asbestos, or other hazardous substances, requiring careful assessment before use.

The Case for New Sustainable Materials

New materials designed for sustainability can offer modern efficiency and eco-conscious production methods. These are particularly useful for homeowners looking for specific styles or performance guarantees.

Pros:

- **Consistency and Reliability:** New sustainable materials meet modern building standards and are free from hazardous substances.
- **Innovative Eco-Friendly Technologies:** Many newer materials incorporate recycled content, low-VOC finishes, and energy-efficient production methods.
- **Easier to Work With:** Unlike reclaimed materials, which may require extra processing, new sustainable materials come ready to install.
- **More Choices:** From bamboo flooring to FSC-certified wood, new sustainable materials come in a variety of styles, colors, and finishes.

Cons:

- **Higher Cost:** Many eco-friendly materials come at a premium compared to standard options.
- **Resource Use:** Even sustainable new materials require energy and resources to produce and transport.
- **Less Character:** New materials may lack the unique aesthetic of reclaimed wood or repurposed fixtures.

Finding the Right Balance

The decision between reclaimed and new materials doesn't have to be all-or-nothing. Many homeowners find success in mixing both—using reclaimed wood for accent walls or furniture while choosing new sustainable tiles or countertops. The key is to assess your renovation needs, budget, and design preferences while keeping sustainability in focus.

Section 3: VOC-Free Paints and Finishes (And Why They Matter for Your Health)

When renovating a home sustainably, one of the most important yet often overlooked choices is the type of paint and finishes used. Traditional paints and finishes contain volatile organic compounds (VOCs), which can have serious consequences for indoor air quality and personal health. Fortunately, VOC-free alternatives exist that offer both environmental benefits and a healthier living space.

Understanding VOCs and Their Impact

Volatile organic compounds (VOCs) are chemicals that easily become airborne at room temperature. They are commonly found in paints, stains, sealants, and varnishes. While the fresh smell of paint may seem harmless, it's actually a sign of VOCs being released into the air—a process known as off-gassing.

Exposure to VOCs can cause headaches, dizziness, respiratory problems, and even long-term health issues like liver and kidney damage. Children, pregnant women, and individuals with asthma or allergies are particularly sensitive to VOC exposure. Over time, these chemicals contribute to indoor air pollution, making the air inside a home more toxic than the air outside.

The Benefits of VOC-Free Paints and Finishes

Opting for VOC-free or low-VOC paints and finishes can significantly improve indoor air quality. Here are some key advantages:

- **Healthier Living Environment:** Since these paints don't release harmful fumes, they help reduce

respiratory issues, allergic reactions, and potential long-term health risks.
- **Eco-Friendly:** Traditional paints contribute to air pollution, while VOC-free alternatives minimize environmental harm.
- **Low Odor:** Unlike regular paints that leave a strong chemical smell, VOC-free options have a much milder or even odorless application.
- **Durability and Quality:** Advances in paint technology have led to VOC-free options that offer excellent coverage, long-lasting finishes, and resistance to stains and moisture.

How to Identify Truly VOC-Free Products

Not all "low-VOC" or "green" paints are truly free of harmful chemicals. Here's how to ensure you're getting the best option:

- **Check Certifications:** Look for third-party certifications such as Green Seal, Greenguard, or the EPA's Safer Choice label.
- **Read the Fine Print:** Some brands market their products as "low-VOC," but they may still contain harmful chemicals. Check the ingredients list and VOC content level.
- **Opt for Water-Based Over Oil-Based:** Water-based paints and finishes generally have lower VOC levels than oil-based alternatives.
- **Avoid Additional Toxic Additives:** Some paints may be VOC-free but still contain other harmful substances like biocides, fungicides, and heavy metals.

Choosing the Right VOC-Free Paint for Your Home

When selecting a VOC-free paint, consider the following factors:

- **Finish Type:** Matte, eggshell, semi-gloss, and high-gloss options are available in VOC-free varieties. Choose a finish that suits the needs of each room.
- **Color Selection:** Some eco-friendly paints offer fewer color choices, but many brands now provide a wide variety of shades.
- **Application Process:** VOC-free paints often require proper priming and multiple coats for the best results. Be sure to follow manufacturer instructions.

VOC-Free Finishes: Stains, Sealants, and Varnishes

Beyond paint, other home finishes such as stains, sealants, and varnishes also contain VOCs. When selecting these materials, look for natural or water-based alternatives:

- **Plant-Based Wood Stains:** Made from natural oils and waxes, these stains enhance wood's natural beauty without toxic chemicals.
- **Water-Based Sealants:** Ideal for floors, countertops, and furniture, these sealants provide protection without releasing harmful fumes.
- **Beeswax and Natural Oils:** For furniture and woodwork, beeswax and linseed oil offer excellent finishes without the need for synthetic additives.

Switching to VOC-free paints and finishes is a simple yet powerful step toward a sustainable and healthy home renovation. By making this choice, homeowners can enjoy a safer indoor environment while reducing their ecological footprint.

Section 4: Eco-Friendly Flooring Options (Bamboo, Cork, Recycled Wood, etc.)

Flooring is one of the most impactful choices in home renovation. It sets the tone for your space, determines comfort levels, and plays a crucial role in sustainability. Traditional flooring materials, such as conventional hardwood and synthetic carpets, can have a significant environmental impact, from deforestation to chemical-laden manufacturing processes. Fortunately, there are eco-friendly alternatives that not only look beautiful but also contribute positively to the environment.

Why Flooring Matters in Sustainability

Many homeowners don't realize just how much flooring affects their home's overall sustainability. A floor should be durable, made from renewable or recycled materials, and free from harmful chemicals. Sustainable flooring minimizes waste, reduces indoor air pollution, and can even help with energy efficiency by retaining heat or staying cool naturally.

Let's explore some of the most eco-friendly flooring options and what makes them a great choice for a sustainable home renovation.

1. Bamboo Flooring: Strength Meets Sustainability

Bamboo flooring has gained popularity as a sustainable alternative to traditional hardwood. Bamboo is technically a grass, not a tree, which means it grows rapidly—some species can reach maturity in just three to five years compared to hardwood trees that take decades.

Pros of Bamboo Flooring:

- **Rapid Regeneration:** Unlike hardwood, which takes years to replenish, bamboo grows quickly and regenerates after being harvested.
- **Durability:** High-quality bamboo flooring can be as strong as traditional hardwood floors and can last for decades with proper care.
- **Aesthetic Appeal:** Bamboo has a sleek, modern look with natural variations in grain and color.
- **Low VOC Options:** Many bamboo flooring options are now available with low or zero volatile organic compounds (VOCs), making them healthier for indoor air quality.

Cons of Bamboo Flooring:

- **Moisture Sensitivity:** Bamboo can absorb moisture, making it prone to warping in humid or wet environments.
- **Quality Variations:** Some manufacturers use excessive adhesives or chemicals in bamboo flooring, so it's essential to choose certified, non-toxic options.
- **Transportation Footprint:** Since most bamboo comes from Asia, its transportation can contribute to carbon emissions.

Best Uses: Bamboo flooring works best in dry areas such as living rooms, bedrooms, and hallways. If installing in kitchens or bathrooms, proper sealing and maintenance are necessary.

2. Cork Flooring: Comfort and Sustainability Combined

Cork flooring is another excellent eco-friendly choice that is gaining traction among homeowners. Cork is harvested from the bark of cork oak trees, which regenerate after harvesting, making it a renewable resource.

Pros of Cork Flooring:

- **Renewable & Biodegradable:** Cork trees aren't cut down; only the bark is stripped, allowing the tree to continue growing.
- **Soft & Comfortable:** Cork provides a cushioned feel underfoot, making it a great choice for areas where you stand for long periods.
- **Natural Insulator:** Cork has excellent insulating properties, helping to maintain comfortable indoor temperatures and reduce energy costs.
- **Mold & Mildew Resistant:** Cork contains natural antimicrobial properties that make it resistant to mold and mildew.
- **Absorbs Sound:** The soft nature of cork makes it great for noise reduction, ideal for apartments and multi-story homes.

Cons of Cork Flooring:

- **Prone to Damage:** Heavy furniture can leave indentations in cork flooring, and it may be susceptible to scratches.
- **Water Sensitivity:** Cork absorbs moisture, so it's not ideal for bathrooms or damp environments unless properly sealed.
- **Fading:** Direct sunlight can cause cork to fade over time.

Best Uses: Cork flooring is great for bedrooms, playrooms, and offices where comfort and insulation are priorities.

3. Reclaimed Wood: Beauty with a Story

Reclaimed wood is one of the most sustainable flooring choices because it repurposes existing materials rather than requiring new trees to be cut down. This type of wood is salvaged from old buildings, barns, and factories, giving it a unique and rustic charm.

Pros of Reclaimed Wood:

- **Environmentally Friendly:** Reduces the demand for newly harvested wood, helping to conserve forests.
- **Unique Aesthetic:** Each plank has a distinct character, with weathered textures and rich colors that add charm to a home.
- **Durability:** Many reclaimed wood options are made from old-growth timber, which is often harder and more durable than newly harvested wood.
- **Versatile:** Available in a variety of styles, from rustic barn wood to refined hardwoods.

Cons of Reclaimed Wood:

- **Limited Availability:** Since it relies on salvaged materials, it may not always be easy to find matching planks.
- **Higher Cost:** Reclaimed wood can be more expensive than new wood due to the processing involved.
- **Potential for Contaminants:** Older wood may contain lead paint, nails, or other contaminants, so it's crucial to source from reputable suppliers who properly treat and clean the wood.

Best Uses: Ideal for living rooms, dining rooms, and other spaces where a rustic or vintage look is desired.

4. Linoleum: The Misunderstood Eco-Friendly Option

Many people confuse linoleum with vinyl, but the two are completely different. Unlike synthetic vinyl, true linoleum is made from natural materials such as linseed oil, wood flour, cork dust, and natural pigments.

Pros of Linoleum Flooring:

- **Sustainable Ingredients:** Made from renewable, biodegradable materials.
- **Durability:** Can last up to 40 years with proper care.
- **Naturally Antimicrobial:** Resists mold and bacteria growth, making it great for allergy sufferers.
- **Variety of Colors & Patterns:** Available in a wide range of designs to fit different aesthetics.

Cons of Linoleum Flooring:

- **Requires Sealing:** Some linoleum floors need periodic sealing to maintain durability.
- **Soft Surface:** Can be dented by heavy furniture.

Best Uses: Suitable for kitchens, hallways, and areas with high foot traffic.

5. Concrete Flooring: Industrial Chic with Sustainability

Concrete flooring is an unexpected yet highly sustainable choice, especially for modern and industrial-style homes. Instead of covering concrete slabs with carpets or wood, many homeowners now choose to polish and seal them for a sleek, contemporary look.

Pros of Concrete Flooring:

- **Durable & Long-Lasting:** Concrete is virtually indestructible when properly sealed.
- **Energy-Efficient:** Concrete retains heat, helping to regulate indoor temperatures.
- **Low Maintenance:** Requires minimal upkeep compared to other flooring types.
- **Versatile Design:** Can be stained, stamped, or polished for different finishes.

Cons of Concrete Flooring:

- **Hard Surface:** Not as comfortable underfoot as cork or wood.
- **Cold in Winter:** Can feel chilly without rugs or radiant heating.
- **Cracking:** May develop cracks over time, though sealing can prevent this.

Best Uses: Works well in basements, kitchens, and modern open-concept spaces.

Final Thoughts

Choosing sustainable flooring is a powerful way to reduce your home's environmental footprint while creating a stylish, comfortable living space. Whether you opt for bamboo's modern appeal, cork's comfort, reclaimed wood's character, linoleum's durability, or concrete's industrial charm, each option offers unique benefits. The key is to balance sustainability, function, and design to find the perfect flooring solution for your needs.

Section 5: Upcycling and Repurposing – Giving Old Materials New Life

Sustainable renovation isn't just about choosing new eco-friendly materials—it's also about making the most of what you already have. Upcycling and repurposing give old materials a fresh purpose, reducing waste and adding unique character to your home. From transforming old doors into headboards to using reclaimed bricks for garden paths, creative reuse can make your renovation both environmentally and aesthetically rewarding.

Why Upcycling Matters

Every year, millions of tons of construction waste end up in landfills. Much of this waste consists of materials that could have been reused with a little creativity. Upcycling reduces the demand for new raw materials, conserves resources, and lowers your carbon footprint. Plus, it allows you to create custom, one-of-a-kind pieces that tell a story in your home. Instead of discarding old furniture, doors, cabinets, or flooring, consider how they can be transformed into something useful and beautiful.

Finding and Choosing Items to Upcycle

If you want to incorporate upcycled elements into your home, start by taking an inventory of what you already have. Look at existing furniture, fixtures, and materials you plan to replace. Sometimes, a simple change—like a fresh coat of paint, new upholstery, or a different hardware set—can breathe new life into an old item.

Other great sources for upcycling materials include:

- **Salvage yards and architectural reclaim stores** – These places offer doors, windows, wood planks, and even hardware from old buildings.
- **Online marketplaces** – Sites like Craigslist, Facebook Marketplace, and Freecycle often have free or low-cost materials.
- **Garage sales and thrift stores** – A great way to find furniture with solid craftsmanship that just needs a little love.
- **Construction site leftovers** – Many builders discard excess materials that you can repurpose.

Creative Upcycling Ideas for Your Home

If you're wondering how to incorporate upcycled elements into your renovation, here are a few inspiring ideas:

- **Reclaimed Wood Beams:** Salvaged wood from barns or old houses can be repurposed into decorative ceiling beams, floating shelves, or custom furniture pieces.
- **Old Doors as Headboards:** If you're replacing doors, consider using them as a rustic headboard or turning them into a unique dining table.
- **Vintage Windows as Room Dividers:** Instead of tossing old window frames, turn them into stylish partitions that allow light to pass through while creating defined spaces.
- **Upcycled Kitchen Cabinets:** Rather than buying new cabinetry, sand and repaint or refinish your existing cabinets for a fresh look.
- **Mason Jar Light Fixtures:** Glass jars can be turned into pendant lighting, giving your kitchen or dining area a charming rustic feel.

- **Salvaged Metal for Accents:** Old metal sheets or pipes can be repurposed into industrial-style furniture or décor elements.
- **Brick and Stone Pathways:** If you're demolishing an old fireplace or patio, reuse the materials to create garden walkways.

DIY vs. Professional Upcycling

Some upcycling projects are perfect for a weekend DIY enthusiast, while others require professional expertise. Simple projects like repainting furniture, building shelves, or converting doors into tables can be done at home with basic tools. However, for complex projects—such as refinishing hardwood floors, reupholstering antique furniture, or repurposing structural materials—it may be best to work with an expert who specializes in restoration.

If you're not particularly handy but love the look of upcycled pieces, consider hiring a local artisan who specializes in reclaimed materials. They can help you design and craft beautiful custom pieces while ensuring the materials are properly treated for durability.

The Financial and Emotional Benefits of Upcycling

Upcycling not only saves materials from the landfill but also saves you money. Buying new furniture, cabinetry, and décor items can be expensive, but repurposing existing pieces often costs far less. You're also likely to end up with higher-quality, solid-wood furniture compared to mass-produced alternatives.

Beyond the financial benefits, upcycling brings a sense of satisfaction. There's something deeply rewarding about transforming discarded materials into something useful and beautiful. Whether you're breathing new life into a family heirloom or rescuing materials from demolition, your home becomes a personal, meaningful space filled with stories.

Chapter 4 Summary: Build Smart, Build Green

Throughout this chapter, we've explored various aspects of choosing sustainable materials for your home renovation. From selecting eco-friendly woods and tiles to understanding the benefits of reclaimed materials, every choice you make can contribute to a greener home.

- **Sustainable Wood, Tiles, and Countertops:** Choosing FSC-certified wood, recycled tiles, and low-impact countertop materials can significantly reduce your renovation's environmental impact.
- **Reclaimed vs. New Materials:** Reclaimed materials offer unique character and reduce waste, while new sustainable options ensure longevity and ethical sourcing.
- **VOC-Free Paints and Finishes:** Avoiding volatile organic compounds improves indoor air quality and supports long-term health.
- **Eco-Friendly Flooring:** Bamboo, cork, recycled wood, and other sustainable flooring choices offer durability and beauty while minimizing environmental harm.
- **Upcycling and Repurposing:** Giving old materials a second life helps reduce landfill waste, saves money, and creates a home filled with unique, meaningful elements.

With this knowledge, you're now equipped to make smart, sustainable choices that align with your renovation goals.

Chapter 5: Reducing Waste During Renovation

Section 1: The Problem with Construction Waste (and How to Reduce It)

Renovating your home is exciting. You get to transform your space, improve its functionality, and make it more sustainable. But here's something most people don't think about until they're knee-deep in drywall and discarded materials—the sheer amount of waste generated by home renovations. Construction and demolition waste make up a significant portion of landfill material, contributing to environmental degradation. The good news? With some planning, you can significantly reduce waste while still achieving your dream home.

Understanding Construction Waste

When you tear down walls, replace flooring, or upgrade appliances, a lot of waste is generated. This includes wood scraps, old drywall, insulation, glass, metal, concrete, bricks, and even packaging from new materials. The Environmental Protection Agency (EPA) estimates that millions of tons of construction and demolition waste are produced annually, much of which ends up in landfills.

The environmental impact of this waste is massive. Construction debris not only takes up landfill space but can also release harmful chemicals into the air and water. Additionally, producing new materials requires energy and resources, which contribute to deforestation, air pollution, and carbon emissions.

How Renovation Waste Affects You

Beyond environmental concerns, excessive waste can also affect you personally. The cost of waste disposal can add up quickly, and getting rid of old materials improperly can lead to fines or even legal trouble in some areas. Plus, if you're working on a budget, every bit of wasted material means wasted money. By focusing on waste reduction, you can make your renovation process smoother, more cost-effective, and eco-friendly.

Steps to Reduce Waste Before You Even Begin

One of the best ways to minimize waste is to plan ahead. Before you start swinging a sledgehammer, take the time to assess what materials can be salvaged or repurposed. Here are a few steps to get started:

- **Conduct an inventory**: Before starting demolition, walk through your home and take note of materials that can be reused or donated. Cabinets, doors, fixtures, and even old wood can often be repurposed.
- **Work with contractors who prioritize sustainability**: Some contractors specialize in green renovations and can help minimize waste by using deconstruction techniques instead of full demolition.
- **Create a waste management plan**: Know where your waste is going. Research local recycling programs, donation centers, and salvage yards that accept construction materials.
- **Order materials carefully**: Over-ordering leads to excess waste. Measure carefully and order only what you need.

Smart Demolition: Deconstruct Instead of Destroy

Traditional demolition involves knocking things down and throwing everything into a dumpster. Deconstruction, on the other hand, is a more careful process where materials are removed intact so they can be reused or recycled. This method significantly reduces waste and can even save you money.

For example, instead of smashing old kitchen cabinets, carefully remove them and donate them to a local reuse center. Hardwood flooring can often be refinished instead of replaced. Even bricks and concrete can be repurposed for landscaping or driveways.

Recycling and Donating Materials

Before throwing anything away, consider whether it can be recycled or donated. Many materials can be given a second life, either in your own home or in someone else's. Some common materials that can be reused or recycled include:

- **Wood**: Old wooden beams, flooring, and doors can be repurposed into furniture or décor.
- **Metal**: Copper wiring, steel beams, and aluminum fixtures can often be melted down and reused.
- **Glass**: Windows, mirrors, and even old glass tiles can be salvaged.
- **Appliances**: Working appliances can be donated to charities or resale stores.
- **Fixtures and Hardware**: Light fixtures, doorknobs, and cabinet handles can often find a second home.

The Bottom Line

Renovation waste is a major problem, but it doesn't have to be. With the right mindset and planning, you can drastically reduce waste while saving money and benefiting the environment. By focusing on deconstruction, careful planning, and recycling, you'll make your renovation project more sustainable from the very start.

Section 2: Deconstruction vs. Demolition: Salvaging Materials Wisely

When planning a home renovation, one of the biggest decisions you'll face is whether to demolish or deconstruct. Many homeowners assume that the easiest route is simply tearing down and starting fresh, but in reality, this approach often leads to unnecessary waste and lost opportunities. Deconstruction, on the other hand, is a mindful alternative that not only benefits the environment but can also save you money and give new life to materials that would otherwise end up in a landfill.

Understanding the Difference: Demolition vs. Deconstruction

Traditional demolition is exactly what it sounds like—a quick and forceful teardown of structures, walls, fixtures, and materials. This method is typically used when a homeowner or contractor wants to make way for new construction as fast as possible. It involves heavy machinery, bulldozers, and wrecking balls that rip through walls and foundations, leaving behind massive piles of debris. While it's efficient in terms of time, the environmental impact is staggering. A significant portion of that debris consists of reusable materials like wood, bricks, tiles, glass, and even appliances that end up in landfills.

Deconstruction, on the other hand, is the careful dismantling of a structure to preserve as many materials as possible for reuse or recycling. Instead of smashing through walls with a sledgehammer, a deconstruction team takes apart components piece by piece. Windows, doors, cabinetry, hardwood flooring, plumbing fixtures, and even insulation can be removed intact and repurposed. This method requires more time and labor, but the benefits far outweigh the drawbacks.

Why Choose Deconstruction?

1. **Environmental Benefits**
   - Construction waste accounts for an estimated 30% of all landfill content worldwide. By deconstructing instead of demolishing, you significantly reduce this waste, keeping valuable materials in circulation.
   - It also reduces the demand for new raw materials, cutting down on deforestation, mining, and the carbon footprint associated with manufacturing new construction supplies.
2. **Cost Savings and Potential Tax Benefits**
   - Salvaging materials means you can repurpose them in your own renovation, reducing the need to buy new materials.
   - Many organizations accept donated materials for resale, and you may be eligible for tax deductions if you donate to nonprofits like Habitat for Humanity.
   - If you're hiring professionals, deconstruction labor might initially seem more expensive, but the long-term savings in materials and tax incentives often make it worthwhile.
3. **Preserving High-Quality and Unique Materials**

- Many older homes contain high-quality wood, antique fixtures, and handmade tiles that are difficult (or expensive) to find today. Deconstruction allows you to retain these treasures instead of sending them to a landfill.
- Salvaged materials can add character and history to your home while also aligning with sustainable renovation goals.

How to Approach Deconstruction

If you're considering deconstruction over demolition, there are a few ways to go about it:

- **DIY Salvaging:** If you have the time and tools, you can carefully remove fixtures, doors, and other reusable materials before the major renovation begins.
- **Hire a Deconstruction Team:** Many professional contractors specialize in deconstruction. They can safely dismantle and salvage materials more efficiently than a traditional demolition crew.
- **Partner with Salvage Yards or Nonprofits:** Organizations dedicated to material reuse can sometimes assist in deconstruction efforts and arrange pickups for donations.

What Can Be Salvaged?

A surprising number of materials can be salvaged and reused, including:

- Hardwood flooring
- Doors and windows
- Cabinetry
- Sinks, bathtubs, and toilets

- Light fixtures and ceiling fans
- Bricks and stone
- Metal pipes and fixtures
- Insulation and lumber

By carefully dismantling your home instead of demolishing it, you can dramatically reduce waste while also saving money and preserving the beauty of older, high-quality materials.

Section 3: Recycling and Donating Old Fixtures and Furniture

One of the most overlooked aspects of a home renovation is what happens to the old fixtures and furniture once they're removed. Too often, these materials are sent straight to the landfill, contributing to the growing problem of construction waste. But there's a better way—recycling and donating! Not only does this reduce environmental harm, but it also helps those in need, supports the circular economy, and can even save you money. Let's dive into the practical steps you can take to ensure that your old fixtures and furniture find a second life instead of becoming waste.

Why Recycling and Donating Matter

Before we get into the how-to, it's important to understand why recycling and donating are crucial components of a sustainable renovation.

1. **Reduces Landfill Waste**: Construction and demolition debris account for millions of tons of waste each year. By recycling and donating, you help keep usable materials out of landfills, reducing overall waste.
2. **Conserves Natural Resources**: Many furniture pieces and fixtures contain materials like wood,

metal, and glass, which require energy-intensive processes to produce. Reusing these materials minimizes the need for raw resource extraction.
3. **Helps the Community**: Donating fixtures and furniture can provide affordable materials for low-income families, schools, and community centers. Organizations like Habitat for Humanity's ReStores accept gently used items and resell them to support housing projects.
4. **Tax Benefits**: In many places, donations to charitable organizations can be tax-deductible, providing financial incentives for giving items a second life.
5. **Adds Character and Uniqueness**: Instead of buying all-new materials, integrating salvaged items into your renovation adds a personal and eclectic touch to your home.

What Can Be Recycled or Donated?

Almost anything in a home renovation project can be reused or repurposed. Here are some of the most common items that can be recycled or donated:

- **Doors and Cabinets**: Solid wood doors, kitchen cabinets, and vanities can be refurbished and used in other homes or community projects.
- **Appliances**: Functional appliances like refrigerators, ovens, and washing machines can be donated to charities that support low-income families.
- **Windows and Fixtures**: Old windows, light fixtures, and ceiling fans are often in demand at reuse stores and salvage yards.
- **Flooring Materials**: Hardwood flooring can be reclaimed, refinished, and used again. Even some types of carpeting can be cleaned and repurposed.

- **Furniture**: Dining tables, chairs, sofas, and bookshelves can be donated to thrift stores, shelters, or local nonprofits.
- **Plumbing Fixtures**: Toilets, sinks, bathtubs, and faucets in good condition can be recycled or donated for reuse.
- **Bricks and Concrete**: Salvaged bricks can be used for landscaping projects, and crushed concrete can be repurposed as construction material.
- **Metal Items**: Metal from pipes, radiators, and hardware can often be melted down and recycled.

How to Donate Fixtures and Furniture

Donating requires a bit of planning, but it's well worth the effort. Here's how you can make sure your items go to good use:

1. **Assess the Condition**: Ensure that items are in good working condition and free from serious damage. Many donation centers have guidelines on what they will and won't accept.
2. **Find Local Organizations**: Research charities, thrift stores, and nonprofits in your area that accept used furniture and fixtures. Examples include:
    - Habitat for Humanity ReStores
    - Goodwill
    - Salvation Army
    - Local homeless shelters or domestic violence shelters
    - Schools or churches in need of building materials
3. **Schedule a Pickup**: Some organizations offer free pickup services for large items. If not, plan to transport them yourself or hire a service.

4. **Obtain a Donation Receipt**: If you're donating to a nonprofit, request a receipt for tax deduction purposes.

How to Recycle Old Fixtures and Materials

If an item isn't suitable for donation, recycling is the next best option. Here's how to do it:

1. **Check Local Recycling Programs**: Many cities have drop-off centers or curbside pickup for large items. Check with your local waste management service.
2. **Use Specialty Recyclers**: Some materials, such as drywall and certain plastics, require specialized recycling facilities. Look for businesses that accept construction waste.
3. **Hire a Green Hauling Service**: Some companies specialize in collecting renovation debris and sorting out recyclable materials.
4. **Repurpose Materials Yourself**: Get creative! Use salvaged wood for shelving, repurpose an old door as a tabletop, or turn bricks into garden pathways.

Creative Ways to Upcycle Fixtures and Furniture

If you love DIY projects, consider giving new life to old items instead of recycling or donating them. Here are a few ideas:

- **Turn an old dresser into a bathroom vanity**
- **Refinish and paint kitchen cabinets instead of replacing them**
- **Use reclaimed wood to build bookshelves or picture frames**
- **Transform a clawfoot bathtub into a garden planter**

- **Repurpose old windows into a greenhouse or decorative wall art**
- **Convert an antique door into a headboard**
- **Use salvaged bricks for a patio or walkway**

Overcoming Common Challenges

Recycling and donating may require extra effort, but with a little planning, it's entirely doable. Here's how to handle some common hurdles:

- **Time Constraints**: Many people opt for the quickest disposal method due to time constraints. Plan ahead by scheduling pickups or drop-offs early in the renovation process.
- **Lack of Storage Space**: If you don't have space to store materials before donating or recycling, coordinate with organizations that can take them immediately.
- **Unsure Where to Donate**: A quick internet search or a call to local nonprofits can help you find organizations in need of materials.
- **Transportation Issues**: If you lack the means to transport large items, look for charities that offer free pickup services.

Conclusion: A Win-Win for You and the Planet

Recycling and donating old fixtures and furniture is one of the most effective ways to minimize waste during a renovation. Not only does it reduce the environmental impact of your project, but it also benefits others and even offers potential financial incentives through tax deductions. By taking the extra step to ensure materials are reused, you can feel good knowing that your home renovation is part of a larger movement toward sustainability.

The key takeaway? Before you throw anything away, pause and ask yourself: Can this be donated, recycled, or upcycled? A little extra effort goes a long way in making a positive impact on both your community and the environment.

Section 4: Choosing Modular and Long-Lasting Designs

When planning a sustainable home renovation, one of the most effective ways to reduce waste and minimize environmental impact is by choosing modular and long-lasting designs. Unlike conventional renovation approaches that often lead to excessive material waste and frequent replacements, modular designs promote adaptability, efficiency, and sustainability. This section will explore how opting for modularity and durability in home renovation can contribute to a greener future.

The Case for Modular Design

Modular design involves creating spaces, furniture, and structures that can be easily modified, expanded, or repurposed. Instead of building permanent fixtures that may become obsolete over time, modular designs allow homeowners to adapt their spaces to changing needs without excessive waste.

1. **Flexibility for Future Changes**: Life circumstances change—families grow, work situations evolve, and personal preferences shift. Modular designs provide the flexibility to reconfigure layouts, repurpose spaces, and add new elements without requiring extensive demolition or waste.
2. **Efficiency in Construction**: Modular components are often prefabricated, meaning they are manufactured off-site and assembled quickly on location. This

reduces on-site construction waste and energy use, making the renovation process more efficient.
3. **Ease of Repair and Replacement**: Instead of tearing down entire sections of a home when something breaks or becomes outdated, modular designs allow for targeted replacements. Whether it's a damaged cabinet door, a worn-out tile, or a broken light fixture, individual components can be swapped out without disrupting the entire design.

Choosing Durable Materials That Stand the Test of Time

One of the key principles of sustainable renovation is selecting materials that last for decades rather than years. Investing in durable, high-quality materials may come with a higher upfront cost, but it significantly reduces long-term waste and saves money in the long run.

1. **Natural Stone and Hardwoods**: Materials like granite, marble, and hardwood flooring are known for their longevity. While they require proper care, they often outlast cheaper alternatives and maintain their aesthetic appeal over time.
2. **Reinforced Concrete and Steel Frames**: When renovating structural elements, choosing materials like reinforced concrete or steel can enhance durability and reduce the need for frequent repairs.
3. **Scratch- and Stain-Resistant Surfaces**: Countertops and flooring materials should be chosen with durability in mind. Quartz countertops, porcelain tiles, and treated wood surfaces are excellent options that resist scratches, stains, and moisture damage.
4. **Weather-Resistant Exterior Materials**: For exterior renovations, materials like fiber-cement siding, metal roofing, and brick withstand harsh weather conditions

better than traditional wood or vinyl, reducing the need for frequent replacements.

Modular Kitchens and Bathrooms: Sustainable and Functional

The kitchen and bathroom are two of the most frequently renovated areas in a home, often leading to significant material waste. Choosing modular components in these spaces can extend their lifespan and reduce environmental impact.

1. **Modular Kitchen Cabinets**: Opting for modular kitchen cabinets allows homeowners to replace individual sections without having to redo the entire kitchen. High-quality cabinets made from recycled or sustainably sourced materials add to the eco-friendliness.
2. **Prefabricated Bathroom Units**: Many modern bathrooms feature prefabricated units that can be installed quickly and efficiently. These units are designed for easy maintenance and replacement, reducing the need for extensive demolition during future upgrades.
3. **Interchangeable Fixtures and Fittings**: Swapping out faucets, showerheads, and cabinet handles is an easy way to refresh a space without generating significant waste. Look for fixtures made from recycled metals or sustainably sourced materials.

Designing for Disassembly: A Future-Proof Approach

Sustainable home renovation isn't just about choosing eco-friendly materials—it's also about designing spaces that can be disassembled and repurposed with minimal waste. Designing for disassembly (DfD) is an approach that prioritizes materials and structures that can be easily taken apart and reused.

1. **Bolted vs. Glued Connections**: Using bolts and screws instead of adhesives allows for easier disassembly and reconfiguration.
2. **Recyclable Materials**: Choosing materials that can be recycled at the end of their lifespan—such as metal, glass, and untreated wood—ensures that they won't end up in a landfill.
3. **Modular Flooring Systems**: Instead of traditional glued-down flooring, consider interlocking tiles, floating floors, or click-together planks. These options make it easy to replace damaged sections without discarding the entire floor.

The Long-Term Benefits of Modular and Durable Designs

By embracing modular and long-lasting designs in your home renovation, you are not only reducing waste but also creating a space that is adaptable, cost-effective, and environmentally responsible. Investing in durable materials and future-proof designs minimizes the need for frequent renovations, ultimately saving money and reducing your home's carbon footprint.

Section 5: How to Work with Contractors to Minimize Waste

When embarking on a sustainable renovation, one of the most crucial elements in reducing waste is ensuring that your contractor shares your vision. A well-aligned contractor can help you make eco-friendly choices, reduce unnecessary material waste, and ensure that salvageable materials are repurposed or recycled instead of being sent to a landfill. This section explores strategies for collaborating with contractors to achieve a low-waste renovation.

Finding a Contractor Who Cares About Sustainability

Not all contractors prioritize sustainability, so it's essential to vet potential hires carefully. Here are some ways to find and select an eco-conscious contractor:

1. **Ask About Their Experience with Sustainable Practices**
   Some contractors have experience with green building certifications, such as LEED (Leadership in Energy and Environmental Design). Asking them about previous projects involving waste reduction, salvaging materials, or using eco-friendly products can provide insight into their approach.
2. **Check for Green Certifications**
   Certifications such as LEED, NAHB (National Association of Home Builders) Green Certified, or affiliations with sustainable organizations indicate that the contractor is knowledgeable about eco-friendly renovation practices.
3. **Discuss Their Waste Management Plan**
   A contractor who values sustainability should have a waste management plan in place. They should be able to explain how they handle demolition waste, recycling, and salvaging materials for reuse.
4. **Look at Their Supplier Network**
   Contractors often work with specific suppliers. Ask whether they source materials from reclaimed, recycled, or local providers to minimize environmental impact.

Setting Waste Reduction Goals with Your Contractor

Once you've chosen a contractor who aligns with your sustainability goals, it's time to set clear expectations:

1. **Minimizing Demolition Waste**
   Instead of tearing everything down, discuss selective deconstruction with your contractor. This means carefully dismantling structures so that materials such as wood, doors, cabinets, and fixtures can be reused or donated.
2. **Recycling Materials**
   Ensure that your contractor has a plan for recycling materials like concrete, drywall, metal, and wood. Partnering with a local recycling facility can help divert waste from landfills.
3. **Using Salvaged or Recycled Materials**
   Encourage your contractor to incorporate reclaimed wood, recycled metal, and repurposed fixtures into the renovation to reduce the need for new materials.
4. **Proper Disposal of Hazardous Materials**
   Paints, adhesives, and treated wood can contain harmful chemicals. Make sure your contractor follows safe disposal guidelines and uses non-toxic, VOC-free alternatives whenever possible.

Efficient Material Usage and Ordering

Over-ordering materials is a common cause of waste in renovations. Here's how you and your contractor can minimize it:

1. **Accurate Measurements**
   Careful planning and precise measurements ensure that only the necessary materials are ordered, reducing excess waste.

2. **Batch Ordering**
   Ordering materials in bulk reduces packaging waste and minimizes transportation emissions, making your project more sustainable.
3. **On-Site Inventory Management**
   Keeping track of materials prevents unnecessary reorders and helps use up what's already available before purchasing more.

Encouraging Smart Construction Practices

Construction techniques can either generate excess waste or minimize it. Here are some smart construction practices your contractor should follow:

1. **Prefabrication**
   Using prefabricated materials reduces waste, as they are manufactured precisely to specifications, reducing offcuts and unused materials.
2. **Reuse of Temporary Materials**
   Temporary structures like formwork, scaffolding, and protective covers should be reused rather than discarded after a single use.
3. **On-Site Sorting Stations**
   Establishing designated bins for recyclables, salvageable materials, and waste helps ensure proper disposal and maximizes reuse.

Summing Up Chapter 5: Reducing Waste During Renovation

Reducing waste during a renovation requires careful planning, smart material choices, and a commitment to sustainable construction practices. Throughout this chapter, we explored key strategies for minimizing waste:

1. **Understanding the Problem with Construction Waste** – How much waste traditional renovations generate and why reducing it is crucial.
2. **Deconstruction vs. Demolition** – Salvaging materials instead of sending them to a landfill.
3. **Recycling and Donating Fixtures and Furniture** – Giving old materials new life through reuse and donation.
4. **Choosing Modular and Long-Lasting Designs** – Making choices that prevent waste in the long run.
5. **Working with Contractors to Minimize Waste** – Partnering with eco-conscious professionals and setting clear waste reduction goals.

By applying these principles, your renovation can be both sustainable and cost-effective, ensuring a beautiful home without harming the environment. With careful planning and a thoughtful approach, you can transform your space while minimizing its impact on the planet.

Chapter 6: Smart Home, Sustainable Home

Section 1: How Smart Technology Can Make Your Home Greener

In today's world, technology is evolving at a breathtaking pace, and while much of it focuses on convenience, an exciting shift has emerged—smart technology that also makes our homes more sustainable. A smart home isn't just about having fancy gadgets; it's about using technology to reduce energy consumption, minimize waste, and create an efficient living environment that benefits both the planet and your wallet.

But how exactly does smart technology contribute to a greener home? The answer lies in automation, real-time monitoring, and energy-efficient optimization. When used correctly, smart home technology ensures that resources such as electricity, water, and heating or cooling are only used when necessary, eliminating unnecessary waste and cutting down on your overall consumption.

The Role of Automation in a Sustainable Home

One of the most powerful aspects of smart technology is automation. It allows homeowners to control and schedule their energy usage in ways that weren't possible before. Smart thermostats, for example, learn your daily habits and adjust temperatures accordingly, ensuring that heating or cooling systems aren't running when no one is home. Similarly, smart lighting systems can be programmed to turn off when rooms are unoccupied, reducing unnecessary electricity use.

Automated window shades are another great example. They can be set to open during the day to allow natural sunlight to warm your home in winter and close in the summer to block heat, reducing reliance on heating and cooling systems. By automating everyday household functions, you're making sure that no energy is wasted and that resources are used only when needed.

Smart Sensors: The Invisible Energy Savers

Imagine lights that only turn on when someone enters a room or faucets that automatically shut off after a few seconds of inactivity. These are the small but impactful changes that smart sensors can bring into a home. Smart motion sensors and occupancy detectors work to optimize energy use by ensuring that appliances, lights, and even HVAC systems are only in use when they need to be.

Leak sensors are another great investment in sustainability. A hidden water leak can lead to significant wastage over time, but a smart leak detector can alert you to any issues before they become major problems. This not only helps in conserving water but also prevents expensive damage to your home.

Energy Monitoring: Knowing is Saving

Many homeowners have no idea how much energy individual appliances are consuming. This is where smart energy monitoring systems come into play. These systems provide real-time feedback on electricity usage, allowing you to identify energy-hungry devices and adjust your habits accordingly. For instance, if you notice that an old refrigerator is consuming an excessive amount of power, replacing it with a more energy-efficient model could lead to long-term savings.

Some smart plugs also offer energy monitoring features. They allow you to turn off devices remotely and track how much power each plugged-in appliance is using. By simply identifying and managing energy consumption in your home, you can make small but meaningful changes that add up over time.

The Impact of Smart Technology on Water Conservation

While energy efficiency is a key focus, smart home technology can also help conserve water. Smart irrigation systems are a prime example of this. These systems use weather data and soil moisture levels to determine when and how much to water your garden, ensuring that water isn't wasted on overwatering or unnecessary watering during rainy days.

Similarly, smart showerheads and faucets can track water usage and even adjust water flow to reduce waste. Some even come with temperature presets, preventing excess water use while waiting for the water to reach a comfortable temperature. These small but effective changes contribute to an overall reduction in water waste.

The Financial and Environmental Benefits of a Smart Home

Aside from reducing your environmental impact, integrating smart technology into your home comes with significant financial advantages. A smart thermostat alone can save homeowners hundreds of dollars each year in heating and cooling costs. Smart lighting systems drastically cut down electricity bills, and water-saving devices lead to lower utility expenses.

Moreover, many governments and utility companies offer incentives, rebates, and tax breaks for installing energy-efficient smart home devices. This means that while the initial investment might seem high, the long-term savings make it worthwhile.

Conclusion

A sustainable home isn't just about choosing eco-friendly materials or reducing waste during renovations—it's also about optimizing how your home functions on a daily basis. Smart technology is a powerful tool that allows homeowners to minimize energy and water waste while also enjoying increased convenience and comfort.

Section 2: Home Automation for Energy Savings (Lighting, Climate Control, etc.)

In today's world, technology plays a pivotal role in making our homes more sustainable. The integration of home automation systems has revolutionized the way we control our energy consumption. Smart lighting, intelligent climate control, and automated energy management systems have emerged as powerful tools in the quest for sustainability. These advancements not only reduce energy waste but also enhance convenience and comfort.

The Role of Home Automation in Energy Efficiency

Home automation allows homeowners to have greater control over energy use by utilizing smart systems that adjust settings based on real-time data. The ability to program appliances, lighting, and heating and cooling systems can significantly reduce unnecessary power usage, translating into substantial savings on energy bills. According to the U.S. Department of Energy, smart home technology can help reduce electricity consumption by 10-30%, depending on the level of automation used.

By automating energy-related functions, you can ensure that your home remains energy-efficient without requiring constant manual adjustments. Imagine a home where lights automatically turn off when you leave a room, the thermostat adjusts itself based on your daily schedule, and appliances operate only during off-peak hours to save on electricity costs. This is the power of smart home automation.

Smart Lighting: Intelligent Illumination for Efficiency

Lighting is a major component of home energy use. Traditional incandescent bulbs are notorious for wasting energy, while smart lighting systems offer a more efficient alternative. Here's how smart lighting contributes to energy savings:

- **LED Smart Bulbs**: LED bulbs use up to 80% less energy than incandescent bulbs and last significantly longer. When integrated with smart home systems, they can be programmed to turn off automatically when not in use.
- **Motion Sensors and Timers**: Many smart lighting systems come with motion detectors and timers, ensuring that lights are only on when needed.
- **Dimming Capabilities**: Smart bulbs and fixtures often feature dimming capabilities, allowing users to adjust brightness levels based on natural light availability.
- **Voice and App Control**: With the rise of smart assistants like Alexa, Google Home, and Siri, controlling lighting via voice commands or smartphone apps has become effortless. This eliminates the need to leave lights on unnecessarily.

By integrating these features, homeowners can experience both energy savings and added convenience.

Smart Climate Control: The Future of Heating and Cooling

Heating and cooling account for nearly half of a home's total energy use. Smart thermostats and HVAC (heating, ventilation, and air conditioning) systems optimize temperature regulation, reducing energy waste. Here's how these systems contribute to energy efficiency:

- **Learning Thermostats**: Devices like the Nest Learning Thermostat analyze household habits and adjust temperature settings automatically based on user preferences and occupancy patterns.
- **Zoned Heating and Cooling**: Smart thermostats allow for zoned climate control, ensuring that energy is only used to heat or cool occupied areas of the home.
- **Remote Access**: Many smart HVAC systems can be controlled remotely, allowing homeowners to adjust temperatures from their smartphones when they are away from home.
- **Weather Adaptation**: Some advanced smart thermostats factor in weather forecasts to optimize energy use, adjusting indoor temperatures in response to external conditions.

By implementing smart climate control, homeowners can maintain optimal comfort while reducing unnecessary energy consumption.

Smart Power Strips and Outlets: Eliminating Phantom Energy Waste

One of the most overlooked sources of energy waste in a home is phantom energy use. Phantom loads occur when electronics consume power even when turned off. Smart power strips and outlets address this issue by automatically cutting power to devices that are not in use.

- **Advanced Power Strips**: These power strips detect when a device is in standby mode and cut off power supply to prevent energy wastage.
- **Smart Outlets**: These allow users to monitor and control plugged-in devices remotely, ensuring that unnecessary appliances aren't left on.
- **Energy Monitoring Features**: Many smart plugs provide insights into real-time energy consumption, enabling users to make informed decisions about energy use.

By replacing traditional power strips with smart alternatives, homeowners can significantly reduce their overall energy consumption without making drastic changes.

Automated Window Treatments for Temperature Control

Another area where home automation plays a crucial role in energy efficiency is in the management of natural light and heat. Automated blinds and smart window films can help regulate indoor temperatures by reducing heat gain in the summer and heat loss in the winter.

- **Motorized Blinds and Shades**: These can be programmed to open and close based on the time of day, outdoor temperatures, or sunlight levels.
- **Smart Glass and Window Films**: Some advanced window technologies allow glass to change its tint automatically to reduce glare and heat buildup.
- **Integration with Smart Thermostats**: Some automated window systems work in tandem with smart thermostats to optimize energy use, adjusting

window coverings to reduce the need for heating or cooling.

By incorporating automated window treatments, homeowners can further enhance energy efficiency and reduce reliance on artificial climate control.

The Cost and ROI of Home Automation

One of the biggest concerns homeowners have about adopting smart home technology is the initial investment. However, the long-term benefits often outweigh the upfront costs. The return on investment (ROI) for home automation can be seen through reduced energy bills, extended appliance lifespans, and increased home value.

- **Lower Energy Bills**: The efficiency gains from smart home technology can lead to savings of hundreds of dollars annually.
- **Extended Lifespan of Appliances**: Automated systems ensure that appliances run efficiently, reducing wear and tear.
- **Increased Home Value**: Homes equipped with smart technology are more attractive to buyers and can command higher resale values.

Many governments and utility companies also offer rebates and incentives for installing energy-efficient smart systems, further reducing costs for homeowners.

Conclusion: A Smart Home is a Sustainable Home

Home automation is a game-changer in the quest for sustainability. By integrating smart lighting, intelligent climate control, energy-efficient appliances, and automated power management, homeowners can significantly reduce their energy consumption while enhancing comfort and convenience.

The beauty of home automation is its scalability—you don't have to transform your entire home overnight. Start with small changes, such as installing smart bulbs or a programmable thermostat, and gradually integrate more automation systems as your budget allows. Over time, these adjustments will result in a more efficient and eco-friendly home.

As technology continues to advance, the possibilities for energy-saving home automation will only expand. By embracing these innovations today, homeowners can enjoy a future where sustainability and convenience go hand in hand.

Section 3: Monitoring Energy and Water Usage with Apps

The old saying goes, "You can't manage what you don't measure." When it comes to creating a sustainable home, knowledge is power. Modern technology has made it easier than ever to track our household energy and water consumption, helping us make informed decisions that lead to conservation and cost savings. With the rise of smart home technology, homeowners can now rely on apps and smart meters to monitor energy and water usage in real time, identify inefficiencies, and adopt eco-friendly habits effortlessly.

Why Monitoring Matters

Imagine getting an electricity bill at the end of the month without having any clue where all that energy went. Was it the heater running too long? The lights left on overnight? Appliances on standby mode silently drawing power? Without precise data, making effective changes is like shooting in the dark.

Monitoring your energy and water usage allows you to:

- Identify wasteful habits and appliances that consume excessive power.
- Reduce unnecessary consumption, lowering utility bills.
- Set conservation goals and track progress.
- Receive real-time alerts about unusual usage patterns or potential issues like leaks.
- Make informed decisions on upgrading to more efficient appliances.

The Rise of Smart Meters and IoT Devices

Many utility companies now provide smart meters, which replace traditional analog meters and provide real-time data on electricity and water usage. Unlike conventional meters that require manual readings, smart meters automatically send data to your utility provider and allow you to track consumption through an app or website.

Beyond utility-provided smart meters, there are a variety of third-party devices that can enhance monitoring, including:

- **Smart Plugs:** These allow you to track the energy consumption of individual devices and remotely control them.
- **Home Energy Monitors:** These connect to your electrical panel and provide detailed analytics on which appliances are using the most power.
- **Smart Leak Detectors:** These alert you to leaks in your plumbing, preventing water waste and damage.

- **Smart Water Flow Monitors:** These track your water usage in real time and help detect inefficiencies.

Top Energy and Water Monitoring Apps

The right app can make a huge difference in how effectively you monitor and manage your home's resource consumption. Here are some of the most popular apps designed to help homeowners reduce waste:

For Energy Monitoring:

1. **Sense Energy Monitor**
   - Connects to your electrical panel and detects energy usage of various appliances.
   - Identifies "phantom loads" (energy used by devices in standby mode).
   - Provides insights on how to optimize usage.
2. **Emporia Energy**
   - Offers real-time monitoring of energy consumption.
   - Tracks trends over time to help you reduce your electricity bill.
   - Alerts you about abnormal spikes in energy use.
3. **Flume Water Monitor**
   - Attaches to your water meter and provides real-time water consumption data.
   - Sends alerts for leaks, helping to prevent water waste.
   - Allows you to set daily, weekly, or monthly water conservation goals.
4. **Neurio Home Energy Monitor**
   - Helps track energy consumption across your entire home.

- Differentiates between appliances to pinpoint energy drains.
- Provides actionable recommendations to reduce energy use.

For Water Monitoring:

1. **Dropcountr**
    - Connects to water utility data to provide personalized conservation tips.
    - Allows homeowners to compare their usage to similar households.
    - Helps detect leaks and unexpected surges in water consumption.
2. **WaterSmart**
    - Works with many water providers to give customers real-time usage updates.
    - Offers tips for reducing water waste.
    - Sends alerts for unusual spikes that might indicate a leak.
3. **AquaTrip**
    - Detects leaks and provides data on water usage habits.
    - Automatically shuts off the water supply in case of major leaks.
    - Ideal for preventing water damage in unoccupied homes.

How to Use These Apps Effectively

Downloading an app is just the first step; the key is to actively use it to make impactful changes. Here's how:

- **Set Baseline Measurements**: Before making any adjustments, track your current energy and water consumption for a month to establish a baseline.

- **Identify Problem Areas**: Use the data to pinpoint where the most energy or water is being wasted.
- **Set Conservation Goals**: Establish realistic goals, such as reducing energy use by 10% or cutting down water consumption by 20%.
- **Take Action**: Unplug devices, switch to LED bulbs, fix leaks, and use energy-efficient appliances based on the insights from your monitoring app.
- **Monitor Progress**: Continuously check the app and adjust habits accordingly to ensure you stay on track.
- **Receive Alerts**: Set up notifications to be alerted about unusual spikes in energy or water use.

Real-Life Success Stories

To illustrate the power of monitoring, consider the case of Sarah, a homeowner who reduced her electricity bill by 25% just by using a smart energy monitor. She discovered that her old refrigerator was consuming far more power than expected, prompting her to replace it with an energy-efficient model. She also realized that her heating system was running longer than necessary, so she adjusted her thermostat settings, leading to significant savings.

Similarly, Jake installed a smart water flow monitor and found that his lawn irrigation system was using excessive water. By adjusting the watering schedule and installing a rain sensor, he cut his water bill in half while keeping his garden healthy.

The Future of Smart Monitoring

With advancements in artificial intelligence and the Internet of Things (IoT), home monitoring is becoming more sophisticated. Future trends include:

- AI-powered assistants that automatically adjust energy and water consumption based on weather patterns and household behavior.
- Smart home integration where all appliances communicate to optimize resource use.
- Blockchain technology for peer-to-peer energy trading, allowing homeowners with solar panels to sell excess energy efficiently.

Conclusion

Monitoring energy and water usage through apps and smart devices is a game-changer for sustainable living. It empowers homeowners with data-driven insights that lead to smarter decisions, lower bills, and a reduced environmental footprint. Whether you're making small changes like unplugging unused devices or major investments in smart home technology, every effort counts.

Section 4: Sustainable Security Systems (Solar-Powered Cameras, etc.)

Security is a crucial aspect of any home, but traditional security systems can be energy-intensive and costly to maintain. Fortunately, modern technology has introduced sustainable security solutions that provide excellent protection while minimizing environmental impact. Homeowners can now invest in solar-powered security cameras, smart locks, and energy-efficient surveillance systems that integrate seamlessly with their eco-friendly living practices. In this section, we explore how sustainable security systems not only safeguard homes but also contribute to a greener future.

The Need for Sustainable Security Systems

Conventional security systems often rely on hardwired connections and continuous power consumption, making them less eco-friendly. Additionally, some surveillance cameras and alarm systems require regular battery replacements, contributing to electronic waste. By switching to sustainable security solutions, homeowners can:

- **Reduce energy consumption** by using renewable power sources like solar energy.
- **Lower their carbon footprint** with eco-friendly materials and energy-efficient designs.
- **Enhance security** with smart features that optimize power usage and improve surveillance.

With advancements in technology, it is now easier than ever to integrate security solutions that are both effective and environmentally responsible.

Solar-Powered Security Cameras: The Future of Home Surveillance

One of the most innovative solutions in sustainable home security is the solar-powered security camera. These cameras harness the power of the sun to operate, eliminating the need for electricity from the grid. They are ideal for homeowners looking to enhance their security without increasing energy bills or relying on fossil fuels.

Benefits of Solar-Powered Security Cameras:

1. **Energy Independence** – These cameras work off solar panels, reducing reliance on traditional power sources.

2. **Cost-Effective** – While the initial cost may be higher, solar cameras eliminate monthly electricity expenses.
3. **Low Maintenance** – No wiring or electrical installation is required, making them easy to set up and maintain.
4. **Remote Monitoring** – Many solar-powered cameras are equipped with Wi-Fi connectivity, allowing homeowners to monitor their property from anywhere using a smartphone or tablet.
5. **Backup Battery Storage** – Most models include rechargeable batteries that store energy, ensuring functionality even during cloudy days or nighttime hours.

Smart Locks and Keyless Entry Systems

Traditional locks and keys are being replaced by smart locks that enhance both convenience and sustainability. These locks use minimal power and integrate with home automation systems for added security.

Advantages of Smart Locks:

- **Battery-Efficient Operation** – Many smart locks use energy-efficient batteries that last for months or even years before needing replacement.
- **Keyless Convenience** – Eliminate the need for physical keys, reducing metal waste from key production.
- **Remote Access** – Homeowners can lock and unlock doors remotely via smartphone apps, reducing the need for duplicate keys.
- **Integration with Smart Home Systems** – Smart locks work with other eco-friendly devices, such as motion-sensor lighting, to enhance energy savings.

Energy-Efficient Alarm Systems

Home alarm systems provide essential protection, but they can also consume significant amounts of electricity. Sustainable alternatives focus on energy efficiency and advanced monitoring technologies.

Features of Energy-Efficient Alarms:

- **Low-Power Sensors** – Motion detectors and door/window sensors with low-energy requirements extend battery life and reduce power usage.
- **Solar-Powered Sirens** – Solar-powered alarm sirens provide a sustainable alternative to wired alarm systems.
- **Wireless Connectivity** – Many modern alarms use Wi-Fi and mobile networks instead of traditional landlines, reducing the need for extensive wiring and electrical installations.
- **Smart Notifications** – Homeowners receive alerts on their devices, eliminating the need for power-hungry 24/7 monitoring centers.

Smart Lighting for Enhanced Security

Outdoor security lighting is an essential component of home safety, but it can contribute to high energy costs if not managed efficiently. Smart and solar-powered lighting solutions help homeowners maintain security while conserving electricity.

Eco-Friendly Security Lighting Options:

- **Solar Motion-Sensor Lights** – These lights activate only when motion is detected, reducing unnecessary energy consumption.

- **Smart LED Bulbs** – Energy-efficient LED lights last longer and use significantly less power than traditional bulbs.
- **App-Controlled Lighting** – Homeowners can schedule lighting to turn on and off remotely, optimizing energy use.
- **Integration with Security Systems** – Smart lights can work in conjunction with cameras and alarms to enhance security measures.

Eco-Friendly Fencing and Perimeter Security

While security cameras and alarms protect the home from intrusions, perimeter security is equally important. Sustainable fencing materials and eco-friendly security barriers provide both protection and environmental benefits.

Green Perimeter Security Solutions:

- **Bamboo Fencing** – A highly renewable and durable fencing option.
- **Recycled Metal or Composite Fences** – Made from repurposed materials, these fences are sturdy and sustainable.
- **Living Fences (Hedges and Shrubs)** – Natural barriers that provide both privacy and security while contributing to air purification.
- **Motion-Sensor Perimeter Alarms** – Low-energy alarm systems that activate only when movement is detected.

The Role of AI and Machine Learning in Smart Security

Artificial intelligence (AI) is revolutionizing home security by making systems more efficient and proactive. AI-powered cameras and monitoring devices can analyze data in real time, reducing false alarms and improving response times.

AI-Powered Security Features:

- **Facial Recognition Technology** – Identifies known family members and differentiates between intruders and visitors.
- **Predictive Analysis** – AI can learn home routines and detect anomalies, alerting homeowners to potential security threats.
- **Automated Alerts** – Smart systems can notify homeowners and emergency services instantly when suspicious activity is detected.
- **Energy Optimization** – AI adjusts security device settings to minimize energy consumption when not in use.

Making the Transition to Sustainable Security

Adopting sustainable security measures doesn't have to happen all at once. Homeowners can start with small upgrades and gradually integrate more eco-friendly options into their existing systems.

Steps to a Greener Security System:

1. **Assess Current Security Needs** – Identify areas where improvements can be made.
2. **Invest in Solar-Powered Cameras** – Replace wired security cameras with solar-powered alternatives.
3. **Upgrade to Smart Locks** – Transition from traditional locks to keyless, battery-efficient smart locks.

4. **Incorporate Smart Lighting** – Use motion-sensor and app-controlled lighting to reduce unnecessary power usage.
5. **Monitor Energy Consumption** – Use smart apps to track the energy efficiency of security devices.
6. **Expand with AI and Automation** – Integrate AI-powered security features for enhanced efficiency and protection.

Conclusion: A Secure and Sustainable Future

Sustainable security solutions offer homeowners a way to protect their property while reducing environmental impact. By investing in solar-powered cameras, energy-efficient alarm systems, smart locks, and AI-powered surveillance, homeowners can achieve a balance between safety and sustainability. As technology continues to evolve, eco-friendly security options will become even more advanced and accessible, ensuring that the future of home protection is both smart and green.

By making conscious choices today, homeowners can create a secure, sustainable environment for themselves and future generations. Integrating these solutions not only enhances home security but also contributes to a healthier planet, proving that safety and sustainability can go hand in hand.

Section 5: Ethical and Sustainable Tech Brands to Consider

As smart home technology becomes an integral part of sustainable living, choosing the right brands is crucial. Not all companies prioritize sustainability, but some are leading the way in ethical sourcing, energy efficiency, and environmentally friendly practices. This section explores the key aspects of ethical and sustainable tech brands, highlights the best options available, and provides guidance on how to make informed purchasing decisions that align with a green lifestyle.

1. What Makes a Tech Brand Sustainable?

Before diving into specific brands, it's essential to understand what makes a tech company sustainable. Here are some critical factors to consider:

- **Energy Efficiency**: The company produces devices that consume minimal energy, often meeting Energy Star certification.
- **Eco-Friendly Materials**: Products are made from recycled or responsibly sourced materials.
- **Ethical Sourcing**: The company ensures fair labor practices and avoids conflict minerals.
- **Recyclability**: Devices are designed to be easily recyclable or biodegradable at the end of their life cycle.
- **Commitment to Carbon Neutrality**: Companies actively reduce emissions and invest in carbon offset projects.
- **Repairability and Longevity**: Devices are built to last and allow for repairs instead of being disposable.
- **Green Packaging**: Minimal, plastic-free, and recyclable packaging is used.

2. Leading Ethical and Sustainable Tech Brands

1. Google Nest

Google has made significant strides in sustainability. Their **Nest Thermostat**, **Nest Cameras**, and **Nest Hub** devices prioritize energy efficiency and use post-consumer recycled plastics. Google has also committed to running all its data centers and offices on **carbon-free energy by 2030**.

2. Apple

Apple leads the industry in environmental responsibility. The company runs on **100% renewable energy**, and its products—like the **HomePod Mini** and **iPads**—are made using recycled aluminum and responsibly sourced rare earth materials. Apple also has a robust device recycling program through **Apple Trade-In**.

3. Eufy by Anker

Eufy produces smart home security devices, including **solar-powered cameras** and **battery-efficient doorbells**. They design products with longevity in mind, reducing the need for frequent replacements.

4. Signify (Philips Hue)

Signify, the parent company of **Philips Hue**, is a leader in energy-efficient lighting solutions. Their **LED smart bulbs** drastically reduce power consumption, and the company operates on **carbon-neutral** principles.

5. Ecobee

Ecobee's smart thermostats are among the best for **reducing home energy use**. The company also focuses on sustainable manufacturing, and many of their products are made from recycled materials.

6. Fairphone

For those looking for ethical smartphones and tech accessories, Fairphone is a game-changer. Their phones are modular, making them easy to repair, and they use **fairly sourced materials**, ensuring ethical labor practices.

7. Tesla (Solar Products)

While best known for electric cars, Tesla's **solar panels and Powerwall battery storage systems** help homeowners transition to renewable energy, reducing reliance on the grid.

8. IKEA Home Smart

IKEA's **smart lighting, blinds, and energy-efficient products** align with their broader commitment to sustainability. The company is working toward using only **renewable and recycled materials** in its products.

3. How to Choose Ethical Smart Tech for Your Home

When selecting smart home technology, follow these guidelines to ensure your choices are sustainable:

- **Look for Energy Star Certification**: This ensures devices consume minimal power.
- **Opt for Recycled or Sustainable Materials**: Research if the brand uses post-consumer plastics or responsibly sourced metals.
- **Check Repairability Scores**: Platforms like **iFixit** rate products based on how easy they are to repair.
- **Investigate Corporate Policies**: Check the company's commitment to sustainability on their official website.

- **Consider Longevity**: Avoid brands that frequently release new versions of products, pushing planned obsolescence.
- **Review End-of-Life Programs**: Ensure the brand offers trade-in, recycling, or take-back programs.

4. The Future of Sustainable Smart Home Technology

The tech industry is continuously evolving, with new innovations aiming to reduce energy consumption and waste. Some future trends include:

- **Biodegradable Electronics**: Companies are developing devices made from biodegradable materials.
- **Self-Powered Devices**: Smart sensors and gadgets that harness kinetic energy or solar power.
- **AI-Powered Energy Management**: AI-driven smart homes that optimize power usage in real-time.
- **E-Waste Reduction Initiatives**: More brands are developing modular devices for easier repairs and upgrades.

Chapter 6 Summary: Smart Home, Sustainable Home

Throughout this chapter, we explored how integrating smart technology into homes can enhance energy efficiency, improve sustainability, and reduce waste. Here are the key takeaways:

- **Smart technology can significantly lower a home's carbon footprint** by optimizing energy and water use.

- **Home automation**—from lighting to climate control—plays a crucial role in reducing unnecessary energy consumption.
- **Monitoring tools and apps** help homeowners track and manage their energy and water usage more efficiently.
- **Sustainable security systems**, such as solar-powered cameras, contribute to eco-friendly home protection.
- **Choosing ethical and sustainable tech brands** ensures that smart home investments align with a commitment to environmental responsibility.

By integrating sustainable smart home solutions, homeowners can create a **greener, more efficient living space while reducing costs and environmental impact**. The future of home technology is heading towards a **harmonious balance between convenience, security, and sustainability**.

Chapter 7: Indoor Air Quality - Breathing Cleaner at Home

Section 1: Why Indoor Air Pollution Is a Bigger Problem Than You Think

When we think about air pollution, images of smog-filled skies, factory smokestacks, and traffic congestion often come to mind. While outdoor air pollution is a significant concern, many people don't realize that the air inside their homes can be just as harmful—if not more so. Indoor air pollution is an invisible threat, affecting millions of households worldwide. It's not just about dust and pet dander; it includes chemicals from cleaning products, off-gassing from furniture, mold spores, and even toxins released from everyday household items.

The Hidden Dangers Lurking in Your Home

Everyday activities contribute to indoor air pollution, often in ways we don't immediately recognize. Cooking on a gas stove releases nitrogen dioxide, a harmful pollutant linked to respiratory issues. Burning candles and incense can release volatile organic compounds (VOCs) and fine particulate matter into the air. Even something as simple as bringing home a new piece of furniture can introduce formaldehyde, a known carcinogen, into your living space. The issue is compounded by modern homes being more airtight to improve energy efficiency, which can trap pollutants inside with little chance for ventilation.

Common Sources of Indoor Air Pollution

To tackle indoor air pollution, we must first identify where it originates. Here are some of the most common culprits:

1. **Household Cleaning Products:** Many conventional cleaning sprays, disinfectants, and air fresheners contain harmful VOCs that linger in the air long after use.
2. **Furniture and Building Materials:** New carpets, paints, and particleboard furniture release chemicals such as formaldehyde and benzene.
3. **Cooking Emissions:** Frying, grilling, and baking can generate airborne pollutants, particularly when using gas stoves.
4. **Tobacco Smoke:** Even secondhand and thirdhand smoke (residue left on surfaces) can contribute to poor air quality.
5. **Mold and Mildew:** These thrive in damp environments and release spores that trigger allergies and respiratory issues.
6. **Pet Dander and Dust Mites:** Common allergens that can worsen asthma and respiratory conditions.
7. **Pesticides and Insecticides:** Chemical sprays used to combat pests can introduce toxic residues into the home environment.

Understanding these sources is the first step in creating a healthier indoor environment.

The Health Impacts of Poor Indoor Air Quality

Long-term exposure to indoor air pollution can lead to a variety of health issues, from mild discomfort to severe respiratory diseases. Here are some of the most common health effects:

- **Respiratory Issues:** Poor air quality can trigger asthma, bronchitis, and other respiratory conditions, especially in children and older adults.

- **Allergic Reactions:** Dust, mold spores, and pet dander can cause sneezing, watery eyes, and skin irritation.
- **Headaches and Fatigue:** VOCs and carbon monoxide exposure can lead to chronic headaches, dizziness, and fatigue.
- **Cardiovascular Problems:** Prolonged exposure to fine particulate matter has been linked to heart disease and high blood pressure.
- **Increased Risk of Cancer:** Certain airborne chemicals, such as formaldehyde and benzene, have been classified as carcinogens.

Given these potential risks, improving indoor air quality should be a priority for every household.

Why Modern Homes Are at Greater Risk

Older homes had natural ventilation due to their construction methods, which allowed fresh air to circulate more freely. In contrast, modern homes are built with energy efficiency in mind, making them tightly sealed to prevent heat loss. While this is beneficial for lowering energy bills, it also means that indoor pollutants get trapped inside. Without proper ventilation and air filtration, these pollutants accumulate over time, leading to increasingly poor air quality.

The Role of Humidity in Air Quality

Humidity levels play a crucial role in maintaining healthy indoor air. Too much moisture in the air can encourage mold growth and dust mite infestations, while too little humidity can dry out mucous membranes, making residents more susceptible to respiratory infections. Ideally, indoor humidity should be maintained between 30-50% to create a comfortable and healthy environment.

The Connection Between Indoor Air Quality and Mental Health

Beyond physical health, poor indoor air quality can also impact mental well-being. Studies have shown that exposure to airborne pollutants can contribute to cognitive decline, increased stress levels, and poor sleep quality. A well-ventilated, toxin-free environment can improve focus, reduce stress, and promote better overall mental health.

Simple Steps to Improve Indoor Air Quality

While eliminating every pollutant from your home is impossible, taking proactive steps can significantly improve air quality. Here are some quick and effective strategies:

- **Increase Ventilation:** Open windows whenever possible to let fresh air in and pollutants out.
- **Use Air Purifiers:** Invest in a high-quality HEPA air purifier to capture airborne contaminants.
- **Choose Low-VOC Products:** Opt for paints, furniture, and cleaning supplies labeled as low-VOC or VOC-free.
- **Control Humidity Levels:** Use a dehumidifier in damp areas and a humidifier during dry seasons.
- **Regular Cleaning:** Dust, vacuum, and mop floors frequently to reduce allergens.
- **Introduce Indoor Plants:** Certain plants, like spider plants and peace lilies, help absorb toxins from the air.

By understanding the risks and taking proactive steps, homeowners can transform their living spaces into healthier environments for their families.

Section 2: Houseplants That Improve Air Quality

Indoor air pollution is a concern that often goes unnoticed in many homes. While modern homes are built for efficiency, they also trap pollutants inside, leading to poor air quality. Fortunately, nature provides an elegant and effective solution: houseplants. By strategically incorporating plants into your home, you can improve air quality, enhance aesthetics, and promote overall well-being.

How Houseplants Purify the Air

Plants act as natural air purifiers by absorbing carbon dioxide and releasing oxygen through the process of photosynthesis. However, their benefits go far beyond this fundamental function. Many houseplants also remove harmful volatile organic compounds (VOCs) such as benzene, formaldehyde, and trichloroethylene from the air. These toxins originate from furniture, paint, cleaning products, and even electronic devices. Additionally, plants help regulate humidity and reduce airborne dust, making indoor environments healthier.

The ability of houseplants to clean indoor air was first studied in depth by NASA in the 1980s. Their research found that certain plants are highly effective at filtering toxins while simultaneously increasing oxygen levels. By introducing these plants into your home, you can significantly enhance air quality and create a healthier living space.

Top Air-Purifying Houseplants

1. Spider Plant (Chlorophytum comosum)

- **Benefits**: Known for its resilience and low maintenance, the spider plant is highly effective at

removing carbon monoxide, formaldehyde, and xylene from the air.
- **Care**: Thrives in indirect sunlight and requires moderate watering. It also produces small "baby" plants that can be propagated easily.

2. Snake Plant (Sansevieria trifasciata)

- **Benefits**: One of the best plants for filtering toxins such as benzene, formaldehyde, and nitrogen oxides. It also releases oxygen at night, making it ideal for bedrooms.
- **Care**: Extremely low-maintenance, requiring minimal water and surviving well in both low and bright light conditions.

3. Peace Lily (Spathiphyllum spp.)

- **Benefits**: Excellent at removing ammonia, benzene, and formaldehyde. Its beautiful white flowers add aesthetic appeal to any room.
- **Care**: Prefers indirect light and consistently moist soil. Be cautious as it can be toxic to pets if ingested.

4. Aloe Vera (Aloe barbadensis miller)

- **Benefits**: Not only does it filter formaldehyde and benzene, but its gel is also a natural remedy for burns and skin irritation.
- **Care**: Thrives in bright, indirect sunlight and requires minimal watering.

5. Boston Fern (Nephrolepis exaltata)

- **Benefits**: A natural humidifier that removes formaldehyde and xylene from the air, making it perfect for dry environments.
- **Care**: Requires consistent moisture and indirect sunlight.

6. Bamboo Palm (Chamaedorea seifrizii)

- **Benefits**: Effectively removes airborne toxins and adds humidity to dry indoor spaces.
- **Care**: Prefers indirect light and moist soil, but can tolerate lower light conditions.

7. Rubber Plant (Ficus elastica)

- **Benefits**: Known for its ability to remove toxins like formaldehyde, rubber plants also increase oxygen levels in indoor environments.
- **Care**: Prefers bright, indirect light and requires minimal watering.

8. Areca Palm (Dypsis lutescens)

- **Benefits**: A powerful air purifier that adds moisture to the air while filtering toxins like xylene and formaldehyde.
- **Care**: Requires bright, indirect light and regular watering.

9. Golden Pothos (Epipremnum aureum)

- **Benefits**: One of the easiest plants to care for, pothos is highly effective at removing benzene, formaldehyde, and carbon monoxide.
- **Care**: Thrives in a variety of lighting conditions and needs occasional watering.

10. Dracaena (Dracaena spp.)

- **Benefits**: Removes pollutants such as trichloroethylene, xylene, and formaldehyde.
- **Care**: Requires moderate light and watering but can adapt to various conditions.

Arranging Plants for Maximum Air Purification

To achieve optimal air purification, consider placing at least one plant per 100 square feet of living space. Distribute them strategically in areas where air circulation is limited, such as corners, hallways, and bedrooms. Grouping plants together can also enhance their ability to clean the air by creating a more significant impact on localized humidity and toxin absorption.

Here are some suggestions for plant placement:

- **Living Room**: Place a combination of bamboo palms, rubber plants, and snake plants to maintain fresh air and a relaxing atmosphere.
- **Bedroom**: Use a snake plant and peace lily to improve nighttime oxygen levels and promote better sleep.
- **Kitchen**: Aloe vera and golden pothos are great choices for filtering out toxins from cooking fumes and cleaning products.

- **Bathroom**: Boston ferns and peace lilies thrive in humid conditions and help reduce mold spores.

Additional Benefits of Indoor Plants

Beyond air purification, houseplants contribute to mental well-being. Studies have shown that plants can reduce stress, increase productivity, and boost mood. They also create a sense of calm and connection to nature, which is particularly beneficial for individuals living in urban areas with limited access to green spaces.

Moreover, plants contribute to interior design by adding natural beauty and texture. Whether you prefer a minimalist aesthetic or a jungle-like ambiance, incorporating greenery can enhance the visual appeal of any home.

Caring for Houseplants

To ensure your houseplants thrive, follow these basic care tips:

- **Light**: Understand the lighting needs of each plant and place them accordingly.
- **Watering**: Avoid overwatering, as most houseplants do not tolerate waterlogged soil.
- **Humidity**: Some plants, such as ferns and palms, require higher humidity levels. Use a humidifier or mist the leaves occasionally.
- **Cleaning**: Dust leaves regularly to allow for better photosynthesis and air filtration.
- **Repotting**: Refresh soil and repot plants when they outgrow their containers.

Conclusion

Houseplants offer a natural and aesthetically pleasing way to improve indoor air quality. By selecting the right plants, arranging them effectively, and providing proper care, you can create a healthier home environment. Not only do these plants filter toxins and regulate humidity, but they also bring a sense of tranquility and connection to nature. Incorporating air-purifying plants into your living space is a simple yet powerful step toward a cleaner, greener home.

Section 3: Natural Cleaning Products (DIY Recipes Included!)

Why Switching to Natural Cleaning Products Matters

Many household cleaning products are packed with chemicals that can degrade indoor air quality, triggering allergies, asthma, and even long-term health problems. Synthetic fragrances, bleach, ammonia, and volatile organic compounds (VOCs) contribute to indoor air pollution, making our homes less healthy. Switching to natural cleaning products not only reduces your exposure to toxins but also helps create a more sustainable and environmentally friendly home.

The good news? You don't need to spend a fortune on store-bought "green" cleaning products. You can make effective, all-natural cleaning solutions at home using simple ingredients like vinegar, baking soda, and essential oils. Let's dive into the world of DIY cleaning and learn how to keep your home spotless while keeping the air fresh and safe to breathe.

The Power of Simple, Natural Ingredients

Before we jump into recipes, let's look at the core ingredients that make natural cleaning products so effective:

- **White Vinegar:** A natural disinfectant and deodorizer that cuts through grease and grime.
- **Baking Soda:** Absorbs odors, acts as a mild abrasive, and neutralizes acids.
- **Lemon Juice:** A natural bleaching agent that also fights bacteria.
- **Castile Soap:** A plant-based soap that cleans without harsh chemicals.
- **Hydrogen Peroxide:** A safer alternative to bleach that disinfects and whitens.
- **Essential Oils:** Natural antimicrobial agents that add pleasant scents.
- **Cornstarch:** Works as a glass and mirror cleaner.
- **Olive or Coconut Oil:** Great for polishing wood and conditioning surfaces.

Now that we understand the basics, let's get into the recipes.

DIY Natural Cleaning Recipes

1. All-Purpose Cleaner

Perfect for countertops, kitchen surfaces, and bathroom sinks.

Ingredients:

- 1 cup white vinegar
- 1 cup water

- 10 drops tea tree or lavender essential oil (for antibacterial properties)

Instructions: Mix all ingredients in a spray bottle and shake well. Spray onto surfaces and wipe clean with a cloth.

---

2. Glass and Mirror Cleaner

Streak-free and chemical-free!

Ingredients:

- 1/2 cup white vinegar
- 1/2 cup water
- 1 tablespoon cornstarch
- 5 drops lemon essential oil

Instructions: Combine all ingredients in a spray bottle. Shake before use and wipe with a microfiber cloth.

---

3. Natural Disinfectant Spray

A safer alternative to harsh disinfectants.

Ingredients:

- 1 cup water
- 1/2 cup hydrogen peroxide
- 20 drops eucalyptus or peppermint essential oil

Instructions: Mix in a spray bottle and shake well. Use on high-touch surfaces like doorknobs and light switches.

4. Toilet Bowl Cleaner

Cleans and deodorizes without toxic fumes.

Ingredients:

- 1/2 cup baking soda
- 1/4 cup white vinegar
- 10 drops tea tree essential oil

Instructions: Sprinkle baking soda into the toilet bowl, add vinegar, and let sit for 10 minutes. Scrub with a toilet brush and flush.

---

5. Natural Floor Cleaner

Works on tile, hardwood, and laminate floors.

Ingredients:

- 1/2 cup white vinegar
- 1 gallon warm water
- 5 drops lavender or lemon essential oil

Instructions: Mix ingredients in a bucket and mop floors as usual.

---

6. Carpet Deodorizer

Removes odors and freshens carpets naturally.

Ingredients:

- 1 cup baking soda
- 10 drops lavender or tea tree essential oil

Instructions: Mix ingredients in a container and sprinkle over carpets. Let sit for 15 minutes before vacuuming.

---

7. Wood Polish

Nourishes and shines wooden furniture.

Ingredients:

- 1/4 cup olive oil
- 1/4 cup white vinegar
- 10 drops lemon essential oil

Instructions: Mix ingredients in a spray bottle, spray onto wood, and buff with a soft cloth.

Making the Switch: Simple Steps for a Natural Cleaning Routine

1. **Declutter Your Cleaning Cabinet:** Get rid of chemical-laden products and replace them with DIY alternatives.
2. **Label Your Homemade Cleaners:** Store your DIY products in clearly labeled bottles to avoid confusion.
3. **Use Microfiber Cloths:** They trap dirt and dust better than paper towels and are reusable.
4. **Adopt a Cleaning Schedule:** Regular maintenance with natural products keeps your home fresh and clean without harsh chemicals.

5. **Educate Your Family:** Make it a team effort by involving everyone in the switch to non-toxic cleaning.

Final Thoughts: A Healthier Home, A Greener Planet

Switching to natural cleaning products isn't just about reducing toxins in your home—it's about making a conscious choice to protect your health and the environment. By using simple, affordable ingredients, you can maintain a clean, fresh home without exposing yourself to harmful chemicals. Plus, DIY cleaners are cost-effective, customizable, and easy to make.

By embracing natural cleaning solutions, you take another step toward a sustainable lifestyle—one that benefits your family and future generations. The air in your home will be fresher, your surfaces just as clean (if not cleaner), and your environmental footprint significantly reduced.

Are you ready to take the leap and ditch chemical cleaners for good? With these DIY recipes and tips, you're well on your way to a healthier, greener home!

Section 4: Choosing Non-Toxic Furniture and Upholstery

When we think about indoor air quality, we often consider factors like air purifiers, ventilation, and natural cleaning products. However, one of the most overlooked contributors to indoor air pollution is furniture. The very couch you lounge on, the bed you sleep in, and the chairs you sit on every day could be quietly releasing toxic chemicals into your home. If you're aiming for a cleaner, greener, and healthier living space, selecting non-toxic furniture and upholstery should be high on your priority list.

Understanding the Hidden Toxins in Furniture

Many conventional furniture pieces contain materials and treatments that release harmful chemicals, known as volatile organic compounds (VOCs). These chemicals evaporate into the air over time, a process called off-gassing, and can cause health issues such as headaches, allergies, respiratory problems, and even long-term conditions like hormone disruption and cancer. Here are some of the common toxins found in traditional furniture:

1. **Formaldehyde** – Used in adhesives for plywood, particleboard, and MDF (medium-density fiberboard), formaldehyde is a known carcinogen.
2. **Flame Retardants** – Common in foam cushions and mattresses, these chemicals have been linked to endocrine disruption and neurological damage.
3. **Stain-Resistant Coatings** – Often applied to upholstery, these coatings contain perfluorinated chemicals (PFCs), which can cause liver and immune system problems.
4. **PVC and Phthalates** – Found in synthetic leather and vinyl furniture, these chemicals are linked to reproductive issues and asthma.
5. **Pesticides** – Used in cotton production, pesticides can leave residues in upholstered fabrics, which may cause skin irritation and other health issues.

Now that we understand the potential risks, let's explore ways to choose safer, eco-friendly alternatives.

How to Identify Non-Toxic Furniture

Choosing furniture that is free from harmful chemicals requires a bit of research, but it's well worth the effort. Here's what to look for:

1. Opt for Solid Wood Over Pressed Wood

Many mass-produced furniture pieces are made from pressed wood products like MDF and particleboard, which contain adhesives that off-gas formaldehyde. Instead, look for furniture made from solid wood, such as oak, maple, walnut, or reclaimed wood. If you must buy composite wood, make sure it is labeled **CARB Phase 2 compliant**, which ensures lower formaldehyde emissions.

2. Choose Natural, Untreated Fabrics

Avoid synthetic fabrics like polyester and vinyl, which are often treated with flame retardants and other chemicals. Instead, look for:

- Organic cotton
- Linen
- Wool (naturally flame-resistant)
- Hemp
- Bamboo fabrics

Check for certifications like **GOTS (Global Organic Textile Standard)** or **OEKO-TEX Standard 100**, which ensure the fabrics are free from harmful chemicals.

3. Go for Natural Latex or Wool Padding

Many cushions and mattresses contain polyurethane foam, which off-gasses VOCs. A healthier alternative is **natural latex**, which comes from rubber trees and contains no harmful synthetic chemicals. Another great option is **wool**, which is naturally flame-resistant and provides excellent breathability.

4. Look for Water-Based and Low-VOC Finishes

Furniture finishes, stains, and paints can release harmful VOCs into your home. Instead, opt for:

- Water-based stains and finishes
- Natural oil finishes like linseed, tung, or walnut oil
- Low-VOC or zero-VOC paints

5. Say No to Chemical Flame Retardants

Flame retardants were widely used in furniture foam, but many have been banned due to health concerns. Look for labels that say **"No added flame retardants"** or check with manufacturers directly. Wool and natural latex are great alternatives since they have inherent fire-resistant properties.

Certifications to Look For

Navigating the world of eco-friendly furniture can be overwhelming, but certifications can help ensure you're making safe choices. Here are some of the most reputable ones:

- **Greenguard Gold Certified** – Ensures that furniture meets strict chemical emissions standards.
- **FSC-Certified (Forest Stewardship Council)** – Ensures that the wood used is sustainably sourced.
- **GOTS (Global Organic Textile Standard)** – Certifies that fabrics are free from toxic pesticides and dyes.
- **OEKO-TEX Standard 100** – Ensures that textiles are free from harmful substances.
- **MADE SAFE Certified** – Guarantees that products are free from toxic chemicals.

Where to Buy Non-Toxic Furniture

Many brands specialize in non-toxic, eco-friendly furniture. Here are a few trusted options:

1. **Avocado Green** – Specializes in organic mattresses and furniture with natural materials.
2. **Medley Home** – Offers solid wood furniture with zero-VOC finishes and natural upholstery.
3. **Maiden Home** – Handcrafted furniture using natural fabrics and sustainable materials.
4. **The Citizenry** – Focuses on ethically sourced, artisan-made furniture.
5. **VivaTerra** – Carries a variety of sustainable furniture and decor options.

DIY Solutions for a Healthier Home

If replacing your furniture isn't an immediate option, there are steps you can take to reduce exposure to toxins in your existing pieces:

1. **Air Out New Furniture** – New furniture often has a strong chemical smell due to off-gassing. Leave it outside or in a well-ventilated area for a few days before bringing it indoors.
2. **Use Non-Toxic Sealants** – You can apply a zero-VOC sealant over pressed wood furniture to reduce off-gassing.
3. **Regularly Clean with Natural Products** – Dust and vacuum frequently to remove chemical residues that accumulate on furniture.
4. **Replace Foam Cushions** – If your couch has old polyurethane foam, consider replacing it with natural latex inserts.

5. **Add Air-Purifying Plants** – Houseplants like snake plants, peace lilies, and Boston ferns can help absorb toxins from the air.

Final Thoughts

Choosing non-toxic furniture and upholstery is one of the most impactful changes you can make to improve indoor air quality. While it may take some research and investment, the long-term benefits to your health and the environment are invaluable. Whether you're replacing one piece at a time or committing to a full home makeover, every step toward a toxin-free home is a step toward a healthier, greener lifestyle.

Section 5: Ventilation Tricks for Fresher Indoor Air

Indoor air quality plays a crucial role in our overall health and well-being. Without proper ventilation, airborne pollutants, allergens, and moisture can accumulate, leading to respiratory issues, mold growth, and an overall decline in indoor air freshness. In this section, we will explore practical ventilation strategies that enhance air circulation, remove indoor contaminants, and create a healthier home environment.

The Importance of Ventilation

Before diving into specific ventilation tricks, it's essential to understand why ventilation matters. A well-ventilated home allows fresh outdoor air to replace stale indoor air, reducing the concentration of pollutants such as volatile organic compounds (VOCs), dust, pet dander, and excess humidity. Proper ventilation also helps regulate indoor temperatures, preventing excessive heat buildup in summer and maintaining comfort during winter.

1. Cross-Ventilation: The Simple Yet Effective Trick

One of the most effective ways to refresh indoor air naturally is through cross-ventilation. This method involves strategically opening windows and doors to create a natural airflow pathway.

- **How to do it:** Open windows on opposite sides of a room or home to allow fresh air to enter while pushing out stagnant air.
- **Best time to apply:** Early mornings and evenings when outdoor air is cooler and cleaner.
- **Enhancing efficiency:** Use window fans to draw fresh air in and exhaust fans to push stale air out.

Cross-ventilation is particularly useful in reducing indoor odors, humidity, and airborne pollutants without relying on mechanical systems.

2. Exhaust Fans: Targeted Airflow Control

Exhaust fans are vital in removing pollutants and moisture from areas prone to high humidity, such as kitchens, bathrooms, and laundry rooms.

- **Kitchen ventilation:** Cooking releases smoke, grease, and odors into the air. A range hood or exhaust fan helps remove these pollutants effectively.
- **Bathroom ventilation:** Showers generate moisture, leading to mold growth. Running an exhaust fan for at least 20 minutes after a shower prevents excess humidity buildup.
- **Laundry room ventilation:** Dryers produce lint and moisture. Ensure proper venting outside to prevent indoor air contamination.

Exhaust fans should be regularly cleaned and maintained to ensure optimal airflow efficiency.

3. Ceiling Fans: Air Circulation on Demand

Ceiling fans help distribute air throughout a room, preventing stagnant air pockets and improving comfort levels.

- **Summer mode:** Set the fan to rotate counterclockwise to create a cooling breeze.
- **Winter mode:** Reverse the rotation to push warm air downward, enhancing heating efficiency.
- **Energy efficiency tip:** Use fans in combination with open windows to enhance ventilation while reducing HVAC reliance.

Ceiling fans improve airflow and complement other ventilation strategies for a well-balanced indoor environment.

4. Whole-House Ventilation Systems

For a more comprehensive approach, whole-house ventilation systems provide continuous fresh air exchange without compromising energy efficiency.

- **Heat Recovery Ventilators (HRVs):** These systems exchange indoor air with outdoor air while recovering heat to maintain energy efficiency.
- **Energy Recovery Ventilators (ERVs):** Similar to HRVs, ERVs also transfer moisture, making them ideal for both humid and dry climates.
- **Smart ventilation controls:** Automated sensors adjust airflow based on indoor air quality levels, ensuring optimal ventilation without energy wastage.

Whole-house ventilation systems are a long-term investment that significantly improves indoor air quality, especially in airtight homes.

5. Natural Ventilation Enhancements

Aside from mechanical solutions, small changes in home design can improve natural ventilation:

- **Transom windows:** Placed above doors, these allow air to flow between rooms even when doors are closed.
- **Vents in interior walls:** Help distribute air evenly throughout the home.
- **Skylights and roof vents:** Facilitate upward airflow, removing hot air naturally.
- **Green walls and trellises:** Plants positioned strategically near windows help filter air and cool indoor spaces.

Enhancing natural airflow not only improves air quality but also reduces energy consumption by minimizing the need for artificial cooling and heating.

6. Air Purifiers and Filters: Supplementing Ventilation

While ventilation is the key to fresher indoor air, using air purifiers and high-quality air filters can enhance the effectiveness of your ventilation strategy.

- **HEPA filters:** Trap fine particles such as pollen, pet dander, and dust mites.
- **Activated carbon filters:** Remove odors, smoke, and VOCs.
- **UV air purifiers:** Eliminate bacteria and viruses in the air.

- **HVAC filter upgrades:** Regularly replacing or upgrading HVAC filters ensures cleaner air circulation throughout the home.

Pairing ventilation with air purification provides an added layer of protection against indoor air contaminants.

7. Reducing Indoor Pollutants at the Source

Good ventilation is essential, but preventing pollutants from accumulating in the first place is just as important. Here are some habits to reduce indoor air contamination:

- **Use non-toxic cleaning products** to avoid chemical fumes.
- **Limit indoor smoking** to prevent harmful residues from circulating.
- **Minimize synthetic air fresheners** and opt for natural alternatives like essential oils.
- **Keep indoor plants** to absorb pollutants and release oxygen.
- **Vacuum and dust frequently** to reduce allergens.

A combination of ventilation and pollutant control ensures long-term air quality improvement.

Summary of Chapter 7: Breathing Cleaner at Home

Indoor air quality is a major but often overlooked aspect of a healthy home. This chapter explored the dangers of indoor air pollution and provided actionable solutions to create a fresher, cleaner indoor environment.

- **Understanding the problem:** Poor indoor air quality can lead to allergies, respiratory issues, and overall discomfort.
- **Houseplants as air purifiers:** Certain plants, such as peace lilies, snake plants, and spider plants, help filter toxins from the air naturally.
- **DIY natural cleaning solutions:** Switching to homemade cleaning products reduces exposure to harmful chemicals.
- **Non-toxic furniture choices:** Selecting upholstery and furniture made from natural, VOC-free materials contributes to a healthier home.
- **Ventilation strategies:** Cross-ventilation, exhaust fans, whole-house systems, and ceiling fans all play a role in maintaining fresh air indoors.
- **Air filtration systems:** HEPA filters, activated carbon filters, and HVAC improvements help remove airborne contaminants.
- **Reducing indoor pollutants at the source:** Simple habits like using eco-friendly products, regular cleaning, and avoiding synthetic air fresheners improve air quality significantly.

By implementing these strategies, homeowners can create a living space that promotes better health, reduces pollutants, and ensures clean, breathable air. A home should be a sanctuary, and fresh air is an essential part of that sanctuary.

Chapter 8: Sustainable Kitchens and Bathrooms

Section 1: Eco-Friendly Kitchen Appliances and Fixtures

The kitchen is often considered the heart of the home. It's where families gather, meals are prepared, and conversations flow. But it's also one of the most resource-intensive areas in the house. From energy-guzzling appliances to water-wasting fixtures, kitchens can significantly impact the environment. Fortunately, with the right choices, you can transform your kitchen into a sustainable and energy-efficient space.

The Importance of Sustainable Kitchen Appliances

Kitchen appliances account for a large portion of household energy consumption. Refrigerators, ovens, dishwashers, and microwaves are used daily, making their energy efficiency a critical factor in reducing a home's carbon footprint. Choosing Energy Star-rated appliances ensures that your kitchen runs efficiently while conserving energy and water.

Refrigerators: Modern refrigerators are designed with sustainability in mind. Look for models that use advanced insulation, energy-efficient compressors, and smart cooling technologies to maintain optimal temperatures with minimal power use. Consider the size of your refrigerator as well; a model that's too large for your needs will waste energy.

Dishwashers: Newer dishwashers use significantly less water than handwashing, especially when used with the eco-cycle function. Look for models with soil sensors that adjust water usage based on how dirty the dishes are, as well as those with shorter cycles to save both water and electricity.

Ovens and Stoves: Induction cooktops are among the most energy-efficient cooking appliances available. Unlike traditional gas or electric stoves, induction cooktops use electromagnetic energy to heat cookware directly, reducing energy loss and cooking time. If you prefer a gas stove, opt for models with sealed burners to minimize heat loss.

Microwaves and Toaster Ovens: Microwaves and toaster ovens use significantly less energy than conventional ovens, making them a smart choice for reheating or cooking small meals. Many modern models have eco-modes that reduce standby energy use when not in operation.

Sustainable Kitchen Fixtures

Beyond appliances, fixtures such as sinks, faucets, and lighting also play a crucial role in creating a sustainable kitchen.

Water-Saving Faucets: Installing aerated or low-flow faucets can cut water usage by up to 50% without compromising functionality. Many modern faucets come with motion sensors, which help reduce water waste by automatically shutting off when not in use.

Eco-Friendly Sinks: Stainless steel and composite granite sinks made from recycled materials are excellent choices for an environmentally friendly kitchen. These materials are durable, long-lasting, and often recyclable at the end of their lifecycle.

LED Lighting: Replacing traditional incandescent bulbs with LED lighting can reduce energy consumption by up to 80%. Under-cabinet LED lighting not only enhances the aesthetics of your kitchen but also provides efficient task lighting while using minimal power.

Smart Technology for a Green Kitchen

Integrating smart technology into your kitchen can further improve sustainability. Smart refrigerators track food inventory and expiration dates, helping to reduce food waste. Some models can even suggest recipes based on available ingredients. Smart dishwashers and ovens allow for remote operation, ensuring appliances only run when necessary.

Choosing Sustainable Materials for Countertops and Cabinets

Kitchen renovations provide an excellent opportunity to incorporate eco-friendly materials. Sustainable options include:

- **Bamboo Cabinets:** Bamboo is a rapidly renewable resource that makes for durable and stylish cabinetry.
- **Recycled Glass Countertops:** Made from repurposed glass, these countertops are not only beautiful but also highly durable and environmentally friendly.
- **Reclaimed Wood:** Using reclaimed wood for shelves or cabinets adds character to your kitchen while reducing demand for newly harvested timber.

The Benefits of an Eco-Friendly Kitchen

Investing in sustainable kitchen appliances and fixtures benefits both the environment and your household. Energy-efficient appliances lower electricity bills, water-saving fixtures reduce utility costs, and sustainable materials contribute to a healthier indoor environment by minimizing harmful emissions.

By making conscious choices in your kitchen, you take a significant step toward reducing your environmental impact while creating a functional and beautiful space. Sustainable kitchens are not just a trend—they are the future of responsible homeownership.

Section 2: The Best Materials for Sustainable Countertops and Cabinets

A kitchen or bathroom renovation offers an excellent opportunity to make sustainable choices that can positively impact both the environment and your daily life. One of the most important aspects of a green remodel is selecting sustainable materials for countertops and cabinets. These surfaces are some of the most frequently used in any home, making it essential to choose options that are durable, non-toxic, and environmentally friendly. In this section, we will explore the best materials for sustainable countertops and cabinets, weighing their benefits and how they contribute to a healthier and greener home.

Sustainable Countertop Options

Countertops are the workhorse of a kitchen or bathroom, serving as a surface for food preparation, storage, and other everyday tasks. Traditional countertops made from non-renewable materials like granite or engineered quartz can have a significant environmental footprint due to mining, energy-intensive processing, and transportation. Fortunately, there are several sustainable alternatives that offer both beauty and functionality.

1. Recycled Glass Countertops

Recycled glass countertops are made from crushed glass set in a resin or cement base, giving them a unique, colorful, and eco-friendly aesthetic. The glass used is often sourced from post-consumer or industrial waste, such as old windows, bottles, or glassware, reducing landfill waste.

Pros:

- Highly durable and resistant to stains and scratches.
- Available in a variety of colors and designs.
- Diverts glass waste from landfills.
- Low maintenance and easy to clean.

Cons:

- Some models can be expensive.
- Cement-based versions may require periodic sealing to prevent stains.

2. Bamboo Countertops

Bamboo is one of the fastest-growing renewable resources on the planet, making it an excellent choice for countertops. These countertops offer a warm and natural look, similar to hardwood, and are highly durable when properly sealed.

Pros:

- Rapidly renewable and highly sustainable.
- Naturally antimicrobial, making it ideal for kitchens.
- Lightweight yet strong.

Cons:

- Requires regular sealing to prevent moisture damage.
- Can be susceptible to scratches and dents if not properly maintained.

3. Reclaimed Wood Countertops

Reclaimed wood countertops are made from salvaged wood that has been repurposed from old buildings, barns, or furniture. This prevents trees from being cut down while giving new life to existing materials.

Pros:

- Unique character and rustic aesthetic.
- Reduces demand for new lumber.
- Can be refinished multiple times for longevity.

Cons:

- Requires regular maintenance and sealing.
- Can be prone to scratches and water damage if not properly treated.

4. Recycled Paper Composite Countertops

Made from compressed recycled paper and resin, these countertops offer a surprisingly durable and sustainable alternative. They have a smooth, matte finish and are available in a variety of colors.

Pros:

- Made from recycled materials, reducing waste.
- Heat-resistant and durable.
- Lightweight and easy to install.

Cons:

- Can be prone to scratching over time.

- Requires periodic sealing to maintain water resistance.

5. Stainless Steel Countertops

Though not traditionally considered a "green" material, stainless steel countertops are extremely long-lasting and 100% recyclable. They are commonly used in commercial kitchens due to their durability and easy maintenance.

Pros:

- Fully recyclable and long-lasting.
- Non-porous and resistant to bacteria.
- Heat-resistant and easy to clean.

Cons:

- Can show fingerprints and scratches.
- More expensive than some other options.

Sustainable Cabinet Options

Cabinets make up a significant portion of any kitchen or bathroom, so choosing sustainable materials can have a substantial impact. Many conventional cabinets are made from materials containing formaldehyde and other volatile organic compounds (VOCs) that can off-gas into your home. By selecting eco-friendly cabinet materials, you can create a healthier indoor environment while reducing environmental harm.

1. FSC-Certified Wood Cabinets

The Forest Stewardship Council (FSC) certifies wood that is harvested responsibly, ensuring it comes from sustainably managed forests. FSC-certified cabinets provide a great way to enjoy the beauty of real wood while supporting ethical forestry practices.

Pros:

- Supports responsible forestry and sustainable land use.
- Offers a natural and classic look.
- Available in various wood species and finishes.

Cons:

- Higher cost compared to non-certified wood.
- May require proper sealing to prevent moisture damage.

2. Reclaimed Wood Cabinets

Like reclaimed wood countertops, reclaimed wood cabinets are made from salvaged materials, reducing the demand for new lumber.

Pros:

- Unique character and history.
- Reduces deforestation and waste.
- Can be refinished or repurposed over time.

Cons:

- May require refinishing to remove old paint or finishes.
- Can be pricier due to labor-intensive sourcing.

3. Bamboo Cabinets

Bamboo cabinets are an excellent alternative to traditional hardwood cabinetry. Since bamboo is a grass that grows quickly, it is a more sustainable option compared to slow-growing hardwoods.

Pros:

- Highly renewable and fast-growing.
- Naturally strong and durable.
- Resistant to moisture and pests.

Cons:

- Can be more expensive than traditional wood.
- Requires careful sourcing to ensure it is harvested sustainably.

4. Formaldehyde-Free Plywood or MDF Cabinets

Many conventional cabinets are made with medium-density fiberboard (MDF) or plywood that contains formaldehyde, a known indoor air pollutant. Choosing formaldehyde-free alternatives can help improve indoor air quality.

Pros:

- Reduces exposure to harmful chemicals.
- Available in a variety of finishes.
- More affordable than solid wood.

Cons:

- Still requires proper sealing for moisture resistance.
- Less durable than solid wood or bamboo.

5. Metal Cabinets

Metal cabinets, especially those made from recycled aluminum or steel, are a highly durable and recyclable option.

Pros:

- Long-lasting and fully recyclable.
- Resistant to moisture and pests.
- Modern and industrial aesthetic.

Cons:

- Can be expensive.
- May require additional insulation for noise reduction.

Final Thoughts

Selecting sustainable materials for your countertops and cabinets is a crucial step toward creating an eco-friendly home. By choosing recycled, responsibly sourced, and non-toxic materials, you can significantly reduce your environmental footprint while enjoying a stylish and functional kitchen or bathroom. Whether you opt for recycled glass countertops, FSC-certified wood cabinets, or bamboo alternatives, your choices can contribute to a healthier home and a greener planet.

Section 3: Water-Saving Tips for the Kitchen and Bathroom

Water is a precious resource, yet it is often wasted in our homes, particularly in the kitchen and bathroom. By making conscious choices and adopting simple water-saving techniques, we can significantly reduce our household water consumption without compromising convenience or hygiene.

This section explores practical strategies to help you conserve water while maintaining an efficient and sustainable home.

Understanding Water Waste in Kitchens and Bathrooms

Kitchens and bathrooms account for a significant portion of household water use. Activities like dishwashing, cooking, brushing teeth, showering, and flushing toilets contribute to excessive water consumption. Leaky faucets, inefficient fixtures, and poor water habits further exacerbate the problem. Fortunately, small changes can lead to substantial savings, benefiting both the environment and your utility bills.

Water-Saving Strategies for the Kitchen

1. Upgrade to a Water-Efficient Faucet

Standard kitchen faucets can use up to **2.2 gallons per minute (GPM)**, but water-efficient models reduce flow rates to **1.5 GPM or less**. Installing aerators or switching to a low-flow faucet can help conserve water without affecting performance.

2. Fix Leaks Immediately

A dripping faucet can waste **over 3,000 gallons of water per year**. Regularly inspect your kitchen sink and pipes for leaks, and repair them promptly to prevent unnecessary water loss.

3. Smart Dishwashing Habits

- **Use a Dishwasher**: Modern dishwashers use significantly less water than handwashing. **Energy Star-certified dishwashers** consume around **3-5**

gallons per cycle, whereas handwashing can use up to **27 gallons per load**.
- **Scrape Instead of Rinsing**: Instead of pre-rinsing dishes, scrape food scraps into the trash or compost bin before loading them into the dishwasher.
- **Full Loads Only**: Run the dishwasher only when it is full to maximize efficiency and minimize water waste.

4. Efficient Handwashing Techniques

- Fill one basin with soapy water and another with rinse water instead of letting the tap run continuously.
- Use a sponge or cloth to lather up dishes before rinsing them in one go.

5. Reduce Water Usage in Cooking

- **Steam Vegetables**: Instead of boiling vegetables, steaming them requires less water and preserves nutrients.
- **Reuse Cooking Water**: Water used to boil pasta or vegetables can be repurposed for watering plants once cooled.

6. Install a Foot Pedal or Motion Sensor Faucet

A foot pedal or motion sensor faucet helps control water flow efficiently, preventing wastage while cooking or cleaning.

Water-Saving Strategies for the Bathroom

1. Low-Flow Showerheads

A standard showerhead uses **2.5 GPM**, but low-flow models reduce it to **1.5 GPM or less**, saving thousands of gallons annually. Look for WaterSense-certified showerheads to maximize efficiency.

2. Reduce Shower Time

Cutting shower time by **2-3 minutes** can save over **1,000 gallons of water per year**. Consider using a **shower timer** to track and limit water use.

3. Turn Off the Tap While Brushing or Shaving

Leaving the faucet running while brushing your teeth or shaving can waste **4-6 gallons per minute**. Instead, wet your toothbrush and turn off the tap while brushing, and fill a cup or basin for rinsing.

4. Upgrade to Water-Efficient Toilets

- **Dual-Flush Toilets**: These allow you to use **1.1 gallons for liquid waste** and **1.6 gallons for solid waste**, reducing unnecessary water use.
- **Low-Flow Toilets**: New models use as little as **1.28 gallons per flush**, compared to older toilets that consume **3-5 gallons**.

5. Fix Toilet Leaks

A leaking toilet can waste **200 gallons of water per day**. To test for leaks, add food coloring to the tank—if the color appears in the bowl without flushing, you have a leak that needs fixing.

6. Install Faucet Aerators

Bathroom faucets typically use **2.2 GPM**, but aerators can reduce this to **1.0 GPM**, significantly cutting water consumption while maintaining water pressure.

7. Collect and Reuse Water

- While waiting for hot water to reach the shower, collect cold water in a bucket and use it for watering plants or flushing toilets.
- Consider installing a **greywater system** to reuse lightly used water from sinks and showers for irrigation.

8. Use a Water-Efficient Washing Machine

When upgrading your laundry appliances, choose an **Energy Star-certified washing machine** that uses **less than 15 gallons per load**, compared to older models that can use up to **40 gallons**.

Additional Tips for a Water-Conscious Home

- **Insulate Water Pipes**: This reduces the time needed for hot water to reach taps, minimizing wasted water.
- **Educate Family Members**: Encourage children and family members to adopt water-saving habits.
- **Use Water-Saving Cleaning Methods**: Instead of using excessive water to clean floors, opt for damp mopping or steam cleaning.

- **Landscape Wisely**: Plant drought-resistant vegetation and use mulch to retain soil moisture, reducing outdoor water needs.

Conclusion

By adopting these water-saving strategies in your kitchen and bathroom, you can significantly reduce household water consumption. Small, mindful changes—such as fixing leaks, using efficient fixtures, and practicing smart water habits—can lead to substantial savings. Sustainable water use benefits not only your utility bills but also the environment, ensuring that future generations have access to this vital resource. Every drop counts, and your efforts to conserve water will contribute to a healthier planet and a more sustainable home.

Section 4: Composting and Reducing Food Waste at Home

Introduction

Food waste is one of the most pressing environmental issues today. Every year, millions of tons of food end up in landfills, where it decomposes and releases methane, a greenhouse gas significantly more potent than carbon dioxide. The kitchen is one of the primary areas in the home where food waste occurs, but with the right strategies, households can drastically reduce their waste and even turn scraps into something valuable. Composting is an excellent way to manage food waste sustainably, and small changes in purchasing and storage habits can make a big difference. In this section, we will explore practical ways to minimize food waste and how to compost effectively at home.

Understanding the Impact of Food Waste

Food waste isn't just about what gets thrown away—it's also about the wasted resources used to grow, transport, and prepare food. When we waste food, we also waste:

- **Water**: It takes about 1,800 gallons of water to produce one pound of beef and 39 gallons for a cup of coffee.
- **Energy**: From refrigeration to cooking, energy is used at every stage of food production.
- **Labor**: Farmers, transport workers, and grocery store employees contribute effort to bring food to our tables.

By reducing food waste, households can conserve these valuable resources, save money, and lessen their environmental footprint.

Smart Strategies to Reduce Food Waste

1. Plan Meals and Shop Wisely

One of the most effective ways to reduce food waste is by planning meals in advance and shopping accordingly. Here's how:

- **Make a shopping list**: Before heading to the grocery store, check what you already have and make a list of what you need.
- **Buy only what you need**: Avoid impulse buys and bulk purchases of perishable items unless they can be used before they spoil.
- **Use a "first in, first out" system**: Arrange food items so older products are used first, preventing spoilage.

2. Store Food Properly

Proper storage extends the shelf life of food and prevents premature spoilage:

- **Refrigerate perishables correctly**: Store dairy, meat, and leftovers at the right temperature to prevent bacterial growth.
- **Keep fruits and vegetables fresh**: Some produce releases ethylene gas, which speeds up ripening. Store ethylene-producing fruits (like apples and bananas) separately from sensitive produce (like lettuce and carrots).
- **Use airtight containers**: This helps maintain freshness and prevents contamination.

3. Use Leftovers Creatively

Instead of throwing out leftovers, repurpose them into new meals:

- **Make soups and stews**: Vegetable scraps, bones, and leftovers can be turned into flavorful broths.
- **Create stir-fries**: A mix of different vegetables and proteins can be turned into a delicious meal.
- **Turn stale bread into croutons or breadcrumbs**: Instead of tossing bread, bake it into crunchy toppings for salads and soups.

4. Understand Expiration Dates

Many people discard food based on date labels, but it's important to understand what they mean:

- **"Sell by"**: This is for store inventory and does not indicate safety.

- **"Best by"**: This suggests peak quality but does not mean the food is unsafe after this date.
- **"Use by"**: This is the manufacturer's recommendation for optimal freshness, but many foods are still edible past this date if stored properly.

The Basics of Composting

Composting is an excellent way to handle food scraps, reducing landfill waste and creating nutrient-rich soil. Here's how to get started:

1. **Choose a Composting Method**

There are several composting methods, each suited for different living situations:

- **Backyard composting**: Ideal for homes with outdoor space. A compost bin or pile can handle a variety of organic materials.
- **Vermicomposting (worm composting)**: A great option for apartments or small homes. Red worms break down food scraps quickly.
- **Bokashi composting**: Uses a fermentation process to break down food, including dairy and meat, which traditional composting cannot handle.

2. **Know What to Compost**

A successful compost pile requires a balance of "greens" (nitrogen-rich materials) and "browns" (carbon-rich materials):

- **Greens (Nitrogen)**: Fruit and vegetable scraps, coffee grounds, eggshells, grass clippings.
- **Browns (Carbon)**: Dried leaves, cardboard, paper towels, wood chips.

- **Avoid**: Meat, dairy, greasy foods, and pet waste as they can attract pests and create odors.

3. **Maintain the Compost Pile**

For optimal composting, follow these steps:

- **Aerate regularly**: Turn the compost pile every couple of weeks to introduce oxygen and speed up decomposition.
- **Keep it moist but not soggy**: The compost should feel like a damp sponge.
- **Monitor balance**: Too many greens create a smelly pile, while too many browns slow decomposition.

Benefits of Composting

Composting offers multiple benefits:

- **Reduces landfill waste**: Organic matter in landfills contributes to methane emissions.
- **Enriches soil**: Compost improves soil structure, retains moisture, and provides essential nutrients for plants.
- **Reduces the need for chemical fertilizers**: Compost acts as a natural fertilizer, reducing reliance on synthetic alternatives.

Additional Tips for Reducing Food Waste Beyond the Kitchen

1. **Support Food Rescue Programs**

Many communities have food rescue programs that redistribute surplus food to those in need. Donating excess food is an excellent way to prevent waste and help others.

2. **Grow Your Own Food**

Having a small herb garden or growing vegetables at home reduces the need for store-bought produce, minimizing waste from packaging and transportation.

3. **Teach Children About Food Waste**

Instilling mindful eating habits in children helps create a new generation that values food and resources. Simple activities like cooking together, composting, and discussing waste reduction can make a big impact.

Conclusion

Reducing food waste and composting are essential steps toward creating a more sustainable home. By planning meals, storing food correctly, using leftovers creatively, and understanding expiration labels, households can significantly cut down on waste. Composting provides a natural way to recycle food scraps, enriching soil and reducing methane emissions from landfills. Small, mindful changes in daily habits not only benefit the environment but also save money and resources. Every effort counts, and when combined, these actions can lead to a healthier planet and a more efficient home.

Section 5: Zero-Waste Bathroom Swaps (Bamboo Toothbrushes, Refillable Products, etc.)

Rethinking Your Bathroom Routine: A Zero-Waste Approach

A sustainable home isn't just about the big elements like energy-efficient appliances or eco-friendly flooring. Even the smallest items in your bathroom contribute to the overall waste footprint of your household. From single-use plastic packaging to disposable hygiene products, our bathrooms generate a significant amount of waste. However, with thoughtful choices and a commitment to sustainability, you can transform your bathroom into a nearly zero-waste space.

In this section, we'll explore some simple yet effective zero-waste swaps for everyday bathroom essentials, helping you reduce waste while maintaining convenience and hygiene.

The Problem with Conventional Bathroom Products

Most conventional bathroom products, from toothpaste tubes to shampoo bottles, are designed for convenience rather than sustainability. Here's why they pose a problem:

- **Plastic Packaging**: Most bathroom essentials come in plastic containers, many of which are non-recyclable and end up in landfills or oceans.
- **Chemical Waste**: Many soaps, shampoos, and dental products contain synthetic chemicals that can pollute waterways.
- **Single-Use Items**: Disposable razors, cotton swabs, and makeup remover wipes contribute to the growing issue of plastic pollution.

By switching to zero-waste alternatives, you can drastically cut down on plastic waste while supporting brands that prioritize sustainability.

1. Bamboo Toothbrushes: A Small Swap with a Big Impact

One of the easiest zero-waste swaps you can make is replacing your plastic toothbrush with a bamboo alternative. Bamboo toothbrushes are biodegradable, compostable, and just as effective as plastic ones. Some brands even offer toothbrushes with replaceable heads, further reducing waste.

- **Why Choose Bamboo?**
  - Biodegradable and compostable
  - Naturally antibacterial
  - Durable and lightweight

How to Dispose of Bamboo Toothbrushes:

- Remove the nylon bristles (if applicable) before composting the handle.
- Use the handle as a garden marker or for creative DIY projects before discarding it.

2. Refillable and Plastic-Free Personal Care Products

Many personal care products, such as shampoo, conditioner, and body wash, come in plastic bottles that contribute to landfill waste. Opting for refillable or package-free options is a great way to cut down on single-use plastic.

- **Shampoo & Conditioner Bars**: These solid bars work just like their liquid counterparts but come without plastic packaging. They also last longer, making them cost-effective.
- **Powder or Tablet Toothpaste**: Traditional toothpaste tubes are difficult to recycle. Powder or tablet toothpaste often comes in glass jars or compostable packaging.
- **Refillable Deodorant**: Some brands offer deodorants in refillable metal or paper tubes, reducing waste significantly.
- **Bar Soaps Over Liquid Body Wash**: A high-quality bar soap lasts longer and doesn't require a plastic bottle.

3. Eco-Friendly Shaving Options

Disposable razors contribute significantly to plastic waste, as they are difficult to recycle. Switching to a reusable safety razor is a sustainable and cost-effective alternative.

- **Safety Razors**: Made from stainless steel, these razors use replaceable blades that can be recycled.
- **Electric Razors**: Rechargeable razors last for years and reduce the need for disposable options.

4. Sustainable Feminine Hygiene Products

Traditional feminine hygiene products, such as pads and tampons, create a large amount of waste. Sustainable alternatives include:

- **Menstrual Cups**: These silicone cups are reusable and can last for years.
- **Reusable Cloth Pads**: Washable pads reduce waste and can be used for several years.
- **Period Underwear**: Absorbent underwear designed to replace disposable products.

5. Biodegradable and Reusable Cotton Swabs & Rounds

Cotton swabs and makeup remover pads are often single-use items that end up in landfills. Switching to reusable or biodegradable alternatives helps cut down on waste.

- **Bamboo Cotton Swabs**: These swabs are compostable and a better alternative to plastic ones.
- **Reusable Makeup Remover Pads**: Made from washable fabric, these pads can be used multiple times.

6. Water-Saving Bathroom Practices

In addition to zero-waste products, adopting water-saving habits helps reduce waste.

- **Low-Flow Showerheads & Faucets**: These devices reduce water consumption without compromising water pressure.
- **Turning Off the Tap**: Simple habits like turning off the tap while brushing your teeth can save gallons of water over time.
- **Installing a Dual-Flush Toilet**: This allows you to use less water for liquid waste and more for solid waste, saving significant amounts of water annually.

Conclusion: Building a Sustainable Bathroom Routine

A zero-waste bathroom isn't about making all the changes overnight—it's about gradually swapping out unsustainable products for better alternatives. Every small switch, whether it's using a bamboo toothbrush or opting for package-free soap, contributes to a healthier planet. By incorporating these simple changes into your daily routine, you can significantly reduce waste, conserve resources, and support sustainable brands.

Chapter 8 Summary: Sustainable Kitchens and Bathrooms

In Chapter 8, we explored how to create a sustainable kitchen and bathroom through smart choices and eco-friendly practices. Here are the key takeaways:

- **Eco-Friendly Kitchen Appliances & Fixtures**: Investing in energy-efficient and water-saving appliances can reduce utility bills and carbon footprints.
- **Sustainable Countertops & Cabinets**: Materials like reclaimed wood, bamboo, and recycled glass are excellent alternatives to conventional kitchen and bathroom materials.
- **Water-Saving Tips**: Simple adjustments such as installing low-flow faucets, fixing leaks, and being mindful of water use help conserve water in both the kitchen and bathroom.
- **Composting & Reducing Food Waste**: Creating a composting system at home helps reduce food waste while nourishing plants and gardens.
- **Zero-Waste Bathroom Swaps**: Opting for sustainable products like bamboo toothbrushes, refillable personal care items, and reusable hygiene products minimizes plastic waste and pollution.

Sustainability starts at home, and by making small but impactful changes in our kitchens and bathrooms, we can create a greener, cleaner future. Every conscious decision adds up, making your home a more sustainable and environmentally responsible place to live.

Chapter 9: The Outdoor Space - Making Your Yard Eco-Friendly

Section 1: Sustainable Gardening - Composting, Native Plants, and Organic Gardening

Your outdoor space has the potential to be more than just a patch of greenery—it can be a thriving ecosystem that supports biodiversity, conserves resources, and enhances the overall sustainability of your home. With thoughtful gardening practices such as composting, incorporating native plants, and adopting organic gardening techniques, you can transform your yard into an eco-friendly sanctuary.

The Role of Sustainable Gardening

Sustainable gardening isn't just about growing plants; it's about creating a balanced environment where plants, animals, and people coexist harmoniously. Traditional gardening methods often rely on synthetic fertilizers, pesticides, and excessive water use, which can harm the environment. By shifting towards sustainable practices, you contribute to soil health, conserve water, and support local wildlife while reducing your carbon footprint.

Composting: Turning Waste into Nutrient-Rich Soil

One of the easiest and most effective ways to practice sustainable gardening is composting. This natural process breaks down organic waste into nutrient-rich soil amendments that enhance plant growth while reducing landfill waste.

Why Composting Matters

1. **Reduces Waste** – Organic kitchen scraps and yard waste make up a significant portion of household garbage. Instead of sending them to a landfill, composting transforms these materials into valuable soil.
2. **Improves Soil Health** – Compost enriches the soil by adding essential nutrients, improving its structure, and increasing its ability to retain moisture.
3. **Minimizes Chemical Use** – With nutrient-rich compost, there's less reliance on synthetic fertilizers that can pollute water sources and disrupt ecosystems.

Getting Started with Composting

Composting is simple and requires only a few key ingredients:

- **Green materials**: Fruit and vegetable scraps, coffee grounds, grass clippings
- **Brown materials**: Dry leaves, twigs, cardboard, newspaper
- **Moisture and air**: Keep your compost pile damp and aerated for proper decomposition

You can choose from different composting methods depending on your space and lifestyle:

- **Traditional backyard composting**: A compost bin or pile works well in larger outdoor areas.
- **Vermicomposting**: Using worms to break down organic waste is ideal for smaller spaces or indoor composting.

- **Bokashi composting**: A fermentation method that speeds up decomposition, making it great for urban settings.

Regularly turning your compost pile and balancing green and brown materials ensures a faster and more efficient decomposition process.

Native Plants: The Secret to a Low-Maintenance, Eco-Friendly Yard

Native plants are species that naturally occur in a specific region and have adapted to the local climate, soil, and wildlife. Incorporating native plants in your yard offers multiple environmental and practical benefits.

Why Choose Native Plants?

1. **Water Conservation** – Native plants require less water than exotic species because they are adapted to the local rainfall patterns.
2. **Supports Pollinators and Wildlife** – Many native plants provide nectar, pollen, and seeds that sustain birds, bees, butterflies, and other beneficial insects.
3. **Low Maintenance** – Once established, native plants need minimal fertilizers, pesticides, or intervention to thrive.
4. **Reduces Soil Erosion** – Deep-rooted native plants help prevent soil erosion and improve soil health.

How to Incorporate Native Plants

Start by researching native plant species that thrive in your region. You can visit local botanical gardens, extension offices, or native plant societies for guidance. When designing your landscape:

- Choose a variety of plants that bloom at different times to provide year-round habitat and food for pollinators.
- Group plants with similar water and sunlight needs to create efficient, natural microhabitats.
- Avoid invasive species that can outcompete native flora and disrupt the local ecosystem.

By planting native species, you create a vibrant, self-sustaining garden that enhances biodiversity while requiring less upkeep.

Organic Gardening: A Healthier Approach to Growing Food and Flowers

Organic gardening emphasizes the use of natural processes to cultivate plants without relying on synthetic chemicals. This approach benefits not only your health but also the environment.

Key Principles of Organic Gardening

1. **Building Healthy Soil** – Instead of using synthetic fertilizers, organic gardening relies on compost, manure, and natural amendments like bone meal and rock phosphate to nourish the soil.
2. **Companion Planting** – Planting certain species together can naturally repel pests, enhance growth, and improve soil fertility.
3. **Using Natural Pest Control** – Beneficial insects like ladybugs, praying mantises, and lacewings help

control harmful pests. Homemade sprays using neem oil, garlic, or soap can also be effective.
4. **Crop Rotation** – Rotating crops each season prevents soil depletion and reduces the risk of plant diseases.
5. **Mulching** – Applying organic mulch, such as straw or wood chips, helps retain soil moisture, suppress weeds, and regulate temperature.

Starting Your Organic Garden

Whether you have a backyard, balcony, or even just a few pots indoors, you can grow your own organic produce. Start with easy-to-grow vegetables like tomatoes, lettuce, peppers, and herbs. Raised garden beds or container gardening can also be great options for those with limited space.

If you're interested in fruit-bearing plants, consider dwarf fruit trees or berry bushes that require little maintenance and provide fresh produce year after year.

Conclusion

Sustainable gardening is about working with nature rather than against it. By composting, incorporating native plants, and practicing organic gardening, you create a healthier, more resilient outdoor space that benefits both the environment and your well-being. Small changes in the way you garden can lead to significant positive impacts, making your home a true example of eco-conscious living.

Section 2: Creating a Drought-Resistant Landscape

As climate change continues to impact weather patterns across the globe, many homeowners are facing the challenge of maintaining beautiful outdoor spaces while dealing with water restrictions and prolonged drought conditions. Traditional landscaping methods often rely on water-intensive plants and thirsty lawns, which are not only unsustainable but also expensive to maintain in dry regions. The solution? Drought-resistant landscaping, also known as xeriscaping, which focuses on using minimal water while still creating a lush, vibrant yard. In this section, we will explore how to design a stunning, water-efficient landscape that thrives in arid conditions.

1. Understanding Drought-Resistant Landscaping

Drought-resistant landscaping is all about maximizing the use of natural rainfall while minimizing water consumption. The goal is to create an outdoor space that requires little to no supplemental watering once it is established. This is achieved through careful plant selection, soil enhancement, efficient irrigation techniques, and thoughtful design.

Many people assume that a drought-resistant garden means a barren, cactus-filled yard, but this couldn't be further from the truth. With the right approach, you can cultivate a thriving landscape with diverse plant life, colorful blooms, and lush foliage—without wasting precious water resources.

2. Choosing the Right Plants

One of the key principles of drought-resistant landscaping is selecting plants that are well-adapted to dry conditions. Native plants, in particular, are an excellent choice because they have evolved to thrive in the local climate without excessive watering. Look for species that are:

- **Drought-tolerant:** These plants have deep root systems that allow them to access water stored deep within the soil.
- **Low-maintenance:** Plants that require minimal pruning, fertilization, and pest control will not only save water but also reduce overall upkeep.
- **Pollinator-friendly:** Choosing plants that attract bees, butterflies, and birds can enhance biodiversity and create a healthier ecosystem.

Some excellent drought-resistant plant options include:

- **Succulents and cacti** (e.g., agave, aloe, sedum)
- **Mediterranean herbs** (e.g., rosemary, lavender, thyme)
- **Perennials** (e.g., echinacea, black-eyed susans, yarrow)
- **Ornamental grasses** (e.g., fountain grass, blue fescue, switchgrass)
- **Native shrubs and trees** (e.g., manzanita, redbud, desert willow)

Grouping plants with similar water needs together—known as **hydrozoning**—helps ensure that you are using water as efficiently as possible.

3. Improving Soil Health

Healthy soil is the foundation of any successful drought-resistant landscape. Good soil structure helps retain moisture, improve drainage, and provide essential nutrients to plants. Here's how you can enhance your soil for optimal water retention:

- **Add organic matter:** Incorporate compost, leaf mulch, or aged manure to boost soil health and increase moisture-holding capacity.
- **Use mulch:** A thick layer of mulch (such as wood chips, bark, or gravel) helps regulate soil temperature, suppress weeds, and slow down evaporation.
- **Avoid compacted soil:** Aerate your soil by loosening it with a garden fork or aerator to improve root penetration and water absorption.
- **Choose the right soil mix:** If you are planting succulents or other drought-tolerant plants, consider using sandy or well-draining soil to prevent root rot.

4. Efficient Irrigation Strategies

Even in a drought-resistant landscape, some irrigation may be necessary, especially in the initial establishment phase. However, with smart watering techniques, you can significantly reduce water waste:

- **Drip irrigation:** This system delivers water directly to the roots of plants, reducing evaporation and runoff.
- **Soaker hoses:** These hoses allow water to seep slowly into the soil, providing deep, effective watering.
- **Watering in the early morning or late evening:** Avoiding midday watering prevents excessive

evaporation and helps plants absorb moisture more efficiently.
- **Rainwater harvesting:** Collecting and storing rainwater in barrels or cisterns provides a free, sustainable water source for your landscape.
- **Graywater systems:** Reusing water from sinks, showers, and washing machines (with proper filtration) can help keep your plants hydrated without relying on fresh water.

5. Replacing Traditional Lawns

Lawns are often the biggest water guzzlers in a typical yard. Replacing all or part of your lawn with drought-resistant alternatives can lead to significant water savings. Some great options include:

- **Drought-tolerant ground covers:** Plants like creeping thyme, clover, and ice plant create a lush look without the high water demands of grass.
- **Artificial turf:** Modern artificial grass mimics the look of real grass while eliminating the need for watering, mowing, and fertilizing.
- **Gravel, stone, or wood chips:** Hardscaping elements reduce water usage and add visual interest to your landscape.
- **Meadow-style landscaping:** Replacing lawns with a mix of native wildflowers and grasses creates a beautiful, low-maintenance, and water-efficient yard.

6. Designing for Shade and Wind Protection

Reducing exposure to direct sun and harsh winds can help conserve moisture in your yard. Consider these strategies:

- **Planting shade trees:** Trees like oaks, maples, and mesquite provide natural cooling and reduce evaporation.
- **Using pergolas and shade structures:** These structures can shield plants from excessive heat and help create comfortable outdoor spaces.
- **Creating windbreaks:** Rows of shrubs, hedges, or fences can protect plants from drying winds and reduce water loss.

---

7. Benefits Beyond Water Conservation

Drought-resistant landscaping offers more than just water savings. It also provides:

- **Lower maintenance costs:** With fewer watering, mowing, and fertilizing needs, your outdoor space will be easier to maintain.
- **Enhanced curb appeal:** A thoughtfully designed drought-resistant yard can be just as beautiful—if not more so—than a traditional lawn.
- **Better resilience to climate change:** As temperatures rise and droughts become more frequent, a sustainable landscape will remain green and thriving.
- **Increased biodiversity:** Native plants and pollinator-friendly flowers attract beneficial insects and birds, promoting a healthier ecosystem.

Conclusion

Creating a drought-resistant landscape is a smart, sustainable way to maintain a beautiful yard while conserving water. By selecting the right plants, improving soil health, using efficient irrigation techniques, and rethinking traditional lawns, you can build a resilient, eco-friendly outdoor space that thrives in any climate. Not only will you reduce your water bill and maintenance efforts, but you will also contribute to a healthier planet.

Section 3: Eco-Friendly Outdoor Furniture and Decks

Outdoor spaces are an extension of our homes, providing a place to relax, entertain, and enjoy nature. However, conventional outdoor furniture and decking materials often contribute to environmental degradation through deforestation, pollution, and waste. By choosing sustainable options, we can create beautiful, long-lasting outdoor spaces that are kind to the planet. In this section, we will explore the best materials for eco-friendly outdoor furniture, sustainable decking choices, and maintenance tips for keeping your outdoor space green and durable.

Choosing Sustainable Outdoor Furniture

Outdoor furniture should not only be stylish and comfortable but also made from sustainable materials that minimize environmental impact. Here are some of the best eco-friendly materials to consider:

1. Reclaimed Wood

Reclaimed wood is one of the most sustainable choices for outdoor furniture. It comes from old buildings, barns, and other structures, reducing the need for fresh timber. This prevents deforestation and gives new life to materials that would otherwise go to waste. Reclaimed wood furniture often has a rustic charm and is highly durable when properly treated for outdoor use.

2. FSC-Certified Wood

If you prefer new wood furniture, look for pieces certified by the Forest Stewardship Council (FSC). FSC-certified wood comes from responsibly managed forests that follow sustainable logging practices. Teak, eucalyptus, and acacia are excellent choices for outdoor furniture because they are naturally resistant to weather and pests.

3. Recycled Plastic (HDPE Lumber)

Furniture made from high-density polyethylene (HDPE) lumber, such as recycled plastic milk jugs, is an excellent alternative to traditional plastic furniture. These materials are resistant to moisture, UV rays, and insects, making them highly durable. Companies like POLYWOOD produce stylish outdoor furniture that mimics wood but requires minimal maintenance and does not contribute to deforestation.

4. Bamboo Furniture

Bamboo grows quickly and regenerates without the need for replanting, making it one of the most renewable materials for furniture. Bamboo furniture is lightweight, strong, and naturally resistant to pests. However, ensure that it is treated with non-toxic, weather-resistant finishes to prolong its lifespan outdoors.

5. Metal Furniture (Aluminum & Recycled Steel)

Metal furniture, particularly aluminum and recycled steel, is durable, recyclable, and often made from post-consumer materials. Aluminum is rust-resistant and lightweight, while steel provides strength and stability. Choosing powder-coated finishes instead of traditional paint reduces harmful emissions and enhances longevity.

6. Wicker and Rattan (Synthetic or Natural)

Natural rattan and wicker furniture are biodegradable and sustainable when sourced responsibly. However, synthetic rattan made from recycled plastic can be a more durable and weather-resistant alternative. Look for brands that use recycled polyethylene to create woven outdoor furniture with a lower environmental impact.

7. Upcycled and DIY Furniture

One of the most sustainable ways to furnish your outdoor space is by upcycling old materials into new furniture. Pallets, salvaged wood, and repurposed metal can be creatively transformed into tables, benches, and chairs. DIY projects reduce waste and add a personalized touch to your outdoor setup.

Sustainable Decking Options

A deck is the foundation of many outdoor living spaces, but traditional wood decking contributes to deforestation and requires frequent maintenance. Here are some eco-friendly decking options that offer durability and sustainability:

1. Reclaimed Wood Decking

Reclaimed wood is a great option for decks, offering a unique, weathered appearance while preventing the need for cutting down new trees. It is often sourced from old barns, factories, and warehouses, making it a sustainable and visually appealing choice.

2. Composite Decking

Composite decking is made from a mix of recycled wood fibers and plastic, reducing waste and preventing deforestation. Brands like Trex and TimberTech offer composite decks that mimic the look of wood without the need for staining, sealing, or constant maintenance.

3. FSC-Certified Hardwood Decking

If you prefer natural wood, FSC-certified hardwoods like ipe, cumaru, and garapa are excellent options. These species are extremely dense and resistant to weather, pests, and decay. However, ensure they come from sustainable sources to prevent illegal logging and deforestation.

4. Bamboo Decking

Bamboo decking is gaining popularity as a sustainable alternative to traditional wood. It grows quickly, regenerates naturally, and has a high strength-to-weight ratio. Bamboo decks are highly resistant to moisture and pests when properly treated.

5. Recycled Plastic Decking

Decking made from 100% recycled plastic is another eco-friendly option. It is completely waterproof, resistant to insects, and does not require sealing or staining. While the upfront cost may be higher, its longevity and low maintenance make it a cost-effective choice in the long run.

6. Stone and Concrete Pavers

Natural stone and concrete pavers are long-lasting alternatives to traditional wood decks. Permeable pavers allow water to drain through, reducing runoff and helping maintain soil health. Choosing locally sourced stone minimizes the carbon footprint associated with transportation.

Sustainable Outdoor Furniture and Deck Maintenance

Investing in sustainable furniture and decking is just the first step; maintaining them properly ensures their longevity and reduces waste. Here are some eco-friendly maintenance tips:

1. Use Non-Toxic Sealants and Stains

For wood decks and furniture, choose water-based, low-VOC (volatile organic compounds) stains and sealants. Conventional treatments release harmful chemicals into the air and surrounding soil.

2. Clean with Natural Products

Instead of harsh chemical cleaners, use a mixture of vinegar, baking soda, and water to clean decks and furniture. This reduces environmental pollution and prevents toxic runoff into nearby plants and waterways.

3. Protect with Covers and Shades

Using protective covers or placing furniture under shaded areas extends its lifespan by reducing exposure to rain, UV rays, and extreme temperatures.

4. Repair and Refinish Instead of Replacing

Rather than discarding furniture with minor damage, repair it using eco-friendly adhesives and refinishing techniques. Sanding and restaining wood furniture can give it a fresh look without contributing to waste.

5. Recycle or Repurpose Old Furniture

When it's time to replace outdoor furniture, donate usable pieces to second-hand stores or repurpose materials for new projects. Many manufacturers now offer take-back programs to recycle old furniture responsibly.

Final Thoughts

Creating a sustainable outdoor space goes beyond just choosing eco-friendly furniture and decking. It involves mindful purchasing, responsible maintenance, and reducing waste by repurposing and recycling materials. By opting for durable, ethically sourced materials, we can enjoy beautiful, functional outdoor spaces while minimizing our environmental footprint. Whether you choose reclaimed wood, recycled plastic, or FSC-certified timber, every sustainable decision contributes to a healthier planet and a more responsible way of living.

Section 4: Solar-Powered Outdoor Lighting and Irrigation Systems

The Power of the Sun in Your Yard

Harnessing solar power for your outdoor space is one of the most effective ways to reduce energy consumption while maintaining a beautiful and functional yard. Solar-powered outdoor lighting and irrigation systems provide a sustainable solution that not only lowers electricity costs but also reduces your overall carbon footprint. By taking advantage of the sun's abundant energy, you can create a well-lit, thriving outdoor space that requires minimal maintenance and operates efficiently.

The Benefits of Solar-Powered Outdoor Lighting

Traditional outdoor lighting relies on grid electricity, which contributes to energy waste and higher utility bills. Solar-powered lighting, on the other hand, offers a range of benefits that make it an excellent choice for eco-conscious homeowners.

1. **Energy Efficiency**

Solar lights are powered by photovoltaic cells that absorb sunlight during the day and store it in rechargeable batteries. This energy is then used to power the lights at night. Unlike conventional lighting, solar-powered options do not require ongoing electrical consumption, making them highly energy-efficient.

2. **Cost Savings**

Since solar lights rely on free energy from the sun, they eliminate the need for electrical wiring and reduce long-term costs. While the initial investment may be slightly higher than traditional lighting, the savings on energy bills quickly compensate for the expense.

3. Environmentally Friendly

Switching to solar-powered lighting helps reduce greenhouse gas emissions associated with electricity production. Solar lights do not contribute to pollution or require fossil fuel-generated power, making them a sustainable choice for eco-conscious homeowners.

4. Low Maintenance

Solar lights require minimal upkeep. They automatically turn on at dusk and off at dawn, eliminating the need for manual operation. Most models are designed to withstand various weather conditions, making them a durable and long-lasting option.

5. Easy Installation

Unlike wired lighting systems that require trenching and electrical work, solar lights are easy to install. Simply place them in areas that receive ample sunlight, and they will function efficiently without additional setup.

Types of Solar Outdoor Lighting

Solar-powered lighting comes in various styles and functions, allowing homeowners to customize their outdoor spaces based on their needs and preferences.

1. Pathway and Garden Lights

These small, stake-like lights are perfect for illuminating walkways, driveways, and garden paths. They enhance safety while adding an aesthetic touch to your landscaping.

2. Spotlights and Floodlights

For highlighting specific features like trees, statues, or architectural elements, solar spotlights and floodlights provide bright, focused illumination.

3. String Lights and Decorative Lanterns

Ideal for patios, decks, and outdoor seating areas, solar-powered string lights and lanterns create a warm and inviting ambiance without consuming electricity.

4. Motion-Activated Security Lights

These lights provide extra security by turning on when movement is detected. They are an excellent alternative to traditional wired security lights.

Solar-Powered Irrigation Systems: Watering Your Garden Sustainably

In addition to lighting, solar power can also be used to optimize your irrigation system. Solar-powered irrigation systems help conserve water while ensuring your plants receive the hydration they need.

Why Choose a Solar Irrigation System?

With increasing concerns about water conservation, solar-powered irrigation systems offer a sustainable way to maintain a healthy garden. These systems use solar energy to pump and distribute water efficiently, reducing waste and promoting eco-friendly landscaping.

Key Benefits of Solar Irrigation Systems

1. **Water Conservation** – Solar irrigation systems are designed to deliver water precisely where and when it is needed, preventing overwatering and minimizing runoff.
2. **Reduced Energy Costs** – By using solar energy, these systems eliminate the need for electricity or fuel-powered pumps, reducing energy costs.
3. **Sustainability** – Solar-powered irrigation systems align with sustainable gardening practices by utilizing renewable energy sources.
4. **Remote Operation** – Many modern solar irrigation systems are equipped with smart sensors that allow homeowners to monitor and adjust watering schedules remotely.

Types of Solar-Powered Irrigation Systems

There are various types of solar irrigation systems available, each catering to different landscaping needs.

1. Drip Irrigation Systems

Solar-powered drip irrigation systems deliver water directly to the roots of plants, reducing evaporation and ensuring optimal hydration. These systems are ideal for flower beds, vegetable gardens, and potted plants.

2. Sprinkler Systems

Solar-powered sprinklers work similarly to traditional sprinklers but operate using solar energy. They are great for watering large lawns and landscaped areas.

3. Rainwater Harvesting Systems

Some solar irrigation systems incorporate rainwater harvesting, collecting and storing rainwater for later use. This further reduces reliance on municipal water supplies and promotes sustainability.

4. Smart Irrigation Controllers

Advanced solar irrigation systems come with smart controllers that adjust watering schedules based on weather conditions and soil moisture levels, ensuring efficient water use.

How to Install and Maintain Solar Irrigation and Lighting Systems

Installation Tips for Solar Lights

- Choose locations that receive ample sunlight throughout the day.
- Position lights strategically to maximize illumination and enhance security.
- Regularly clean solar panels to maintain efficiency.
- Replace rechargeable batteries when needed to ensure optimal performance.

Setting Up a Solar Irrigation System

- Determine water needs based on the size and type of your garden.
- Choose an appropriate solar-powered pump that meets your water pressure requirements.
- Install a drip or sprinkler system based on the type of plants in your yard.
- Integrate a smart controller for automated scheduling and efficiency.

Future Trends in Solar-Powered Outdoor Solutions

The advancements in solar technology continue to improve the efficiency and affordability of outdoor solar solutions. Future trends include:

1. **Enhanced Battery Storage** – Innovations in battery technology will allow solar lights and irrigation systems to store more energy and operate longer.
2. **Integrated Smart Features** – AI-driven irrigation systems will optimize water usage by analyzing weather patterns and soil conditions.
3. **Multi-Purpose Solar Devices** – Hybrid systems that combine lighting, security cameras, and irrigation controls in a single unit.

Conclusion: A Greener, Smarter Yard

Switching to solar-powered outdoor lighting and irrigation systems is a significant step toward creating a sustainable, energy-efficient yard. Not only do these systems reduce electricity and water waste, but they also contribute to environmental preservation. By harnessing the power of the sun, you can illuminate your garden, maintain a healthy landscape, and minimize your ecological footprint—all while enjoying the beauty of an eco-friendly outdoor space.

Section 5: Backyard Beekeeping and Other Small-Scale Sustainability Projects

As homeowners look for ways to create an eco-friendly outdoor space, many are turning to small-scale sustainability projects to make their yards more environmentally conscious. One of the most rewarding and beneficial projects is backyard beekeeping, which not only supports declining bee populations but also helps with pollination in your garden. Additionally, other small-scale projects, such as worm composting, rainwater harvesting, and vertical gardening, can contribute to a greener and more self-sufficient outdoor environment. Let's explore these ideas in detail and see how they can help transform your yard into a sustainable haven.

The Importance of Backyard Beekeeping

Bees are vital for the ecosystem, playing a crucial role in pollination, which ensures that plants reproduce and thrive. Without bees, food production would be significantly impacted. Unfortunately, bee populations worldwide are declining due to habitat loss, pesticide use, and climate change. Backyard beekeeping offers a way to support these essential creatures while also reaping benefits for your garden and home.

Getting Started with Backyard Beekeeping

Starting a backyard beekeeping project requires careful planning and knowledge. Here are some essential steps to begin:

1. **Check Local Regulations:** Before setting up a beehive, check your local zoning laws and beekeeping regulations. Some areas have restrictions on hive placement and colony numbers.
2. **Select the Right Hive:** The most common types of hives include the Langstroth hive, the Top Bar hive, and the Warre hive. Each has its advantages, so choose one that suits your space and management style.
3. **Purchase Bees:** You can buy bees from a local beekeeper or order a package from reputable suppliers. Consider native bee species that are well-adapted to your climate.
4. **Provide a Safe Environment:** Position your hive in a sheltered location with ample sunshine and away from high-traffic areas. A water source nearby helps keep your bees hydrated.
5. **Use Natural Beekeeping Methods:** Avoid using chemical treatments and pesticides inside your hive. Instead, focus on organic methods to keep your colony healthy.

The Benefits of Keeping Bees

- **Improved Pollination:** A single bee colony can pollinate thousands of flowers each day, leading to higher crop yields in vegetable and fruit gardens.
- **Fresh Honey Production:** Home-harvested honey is free of additives and pesticides, making it healthier and more sustainable.
- **Beeswax and Other Products:** You can harvest beeswax to make candles, lip balm, and natural skin care products.
- **Educational and Therapeutic Benefits:** Beekeeping provides an opportunity to learn about insect

behavior and ecology while also serving as a relaxing hobby.

Other Small-Scale Sustainability Projects for Your Yard

1. Worm Composting (Vermicomposting)

Worm composting is a great way to reduce kitchen waste and create nutrient-rich soil for your garden. Unlike traditional composting, which requires outdoor space and time for decomposition, vermicomposting allows you to process organic waste quickly with the help of composting worms, such as red wigglers.

- **How to Start:**
    - Set up a worm bin in a cool, shaded location.
    - Add shredded newspaper or cardboard as bedding.
    - Feed your worms fruit and vegetable scraps (avoid citrus and meat products).
    - Harvest the compost after a few months for use in your garden.

2. Rainwater Harvesting

Collecting rainwater reduces dependence on municipal water supplies and lowers your water bill. It can be used for irrigation, flushing toilets, and even drinking if properly filtered.

- **How to Set Up:**
    - Install a rain barrel beneath a downspout to collect water.

- Use a fine mesh screen to prevent debris and mosquitoes from entering.
- Attach a hose or drip irrigation system to distribute the water efficiently.

3. Vertical Gardening

For those with limited yard space, vertical gardening is an innovative solution to grow food and flowers in a compact area. Using trellises, wall planters, and hanging pots, you can create a lush garden on balconies, patios, or small backyards.

- **Best Plants for Vertical Gardens:**
    - Climbing vegetables (tomatoes, peas, beans)
    - Herbs (basil, mint, rosemary)
    - Small fruit-bearing plants (strawberries, dwarf blueberries)

Sustainable Yard Maintenance Tips

Creating a sustainable outdoor space goes beyond just installing eco-friendly features. The way you maintain your yard also impacts the environment. Here are some additional tips to keep your outdoor space eco-friendly:

- **Use Organic Fertilizers and Pesticides:** Avoid synthetic chemicals that can harm beneficial insects and contaminate water sources.
- **Choose Drought-Resistant Plants:** Reduce water usage by selecting plants that thrive in your climate without excessive irrigation.
- **Mulch Your Garden Beds:** Mulching helps retain soil moisture, suppress weeds, and improve soil health.

- **Opt for Hand Tools Over Gas-Powered Equipment:** Rakes, push mowers, and hand shears produce no emissions and are better for the environment.

Chapter 9 Summary

This chapter explored various ways to make your outdoor space more eco-friendly, from sustainable gardening to renewable energy solutions. Here's a recap of the key takeaways:

1. **Sustainable Gardening:** Using composting, native plants, and organic methods to create a healthier yard.
2. **Drought-Resistant Landscaping:** Designing landscapes that require minimal water through xeriscaping and native plant selection.
3. **Eco-Friendly Outdoor Furniture:** Choosing furniture made from recycled or sustainably sourced materials to reduce environmental impact.
4. **Solar-Powered Outdoor Solutions:** Using renewable energy for outdoor lighting and irrigation systems to conserve resources and cut down on electricity use.
5. **Backyard Beekeeping and Small-Scale Sustainability Projects:** Keeping bees, composting with worms, collecting rainwater, and utilizing vertical gardens to promote self-sufficiency and sustainability.

By implementing these practices, homeowners can create an outdoor space that not only benefits the environment but also enhances the beauty and functionality of their yards. Whether it's through pollinator-friendly gardening, reducing water consumption, or repurposing materials, every small step contributes to a healthier planet.

Chapter 10: Living the Green Lifestyle After the Renovation

Section 1: Maintaining Your Sustainable Upgrades

Your home renovation journey may be complete, but living sustainably doesn't end once the last nail is hammered and the final coat of paint dries. A green home is only as effective as the habits and choices you make moving forward. Sustainable upgrades require regular maintenance, mindful usage, and occasional improvements to ensure they continue delivering energy savings, waste reduction, and a healthier indoor environment.

So, how do you ensure that all the eco-friendly features in your home continue to serve their purpose for years to come? Let's explore some practical strategies to maintain and maximize the efficiency of your sustainable home.

1. Keeping Energy-Efficient Systems Running Smoothly

Your home's energy-efficient systems—whether it's solar panels, smart thermostats, or LED lighting—require periodic upkeep to function at peak performance.

- **Solar Panels:** Dust, debris, and bird droppings can reduce the efficiency of solar panels over time. Cleaning them every few months or installing automated solar panel cleaners can ensure they continue generating maximum energy. Additionally, monitoring software provided by most solar companies helps track energy production and spot any drop in performance.

- **Smart Thermostats and Sensors:** Regularly updating the firmware of smart thermostats, occupancy sensors, and automated climate controls ensures they work efficiently. It's also good practice to review usage patterns and adjust settings seasonally to maintain comfort without wasting energy.
- **Energy-Efficient Lighting:** LED bulbs last much longer than traditional incandescent bulbs, but they still need occasional replacement. Checking for flickering or dimming lights can help identify when it's time for an upgrade.

2. Sustainable Heating and Cooling Maintenance

HVAC systems play a critical role in energy consumption and indoor air quality. Here's how to maintain an eco-friendly heating and cooling setup:

- **Regular Filter Changes:** Whether you use a high-efficiency particulate air (HEPA) filter or another eco-friendly alternative, replacing it regularly (every 2-3 months) ensures better air quality and energy efficiency.
- **Annual Inspections:** Have a professional check your heating and cooling systems once a year to ensure they operate efficiently. A small issue left unresolved can lead to increased energy consumption over time.
- **Natural Ventilation:** Continue using natural cooling strategies, such as cross-ventilation, ceiling fans, and well-placed blinds, to reduce reliance on mechanical systems.

3. Water Conservation Upkeep

Water-saving fixtures, such as low-flow faucets, dual-flush toilets, and rainwater harvesting systems, require minimal maintenance but still need occasional checks:

- **Check for Leaks:** A dripping faucet or leaking pipe can waste thousands of gallons of water over time. Inspect plumbing fixtures regularly and repair any leaks immediately.
- **Clean Aerators and Showerheads:** Over time, mineral buildup can clog water-saving aerators and showerheads, reducing efficiency. Soaking them in vinegar once every few months helps maintain water flow.
- **Monitor Rainwater Harvesting Systems:** If your home has a rain barrel or a more advanced water collection system, ensure the filters are clean and the water is being used efficiently for irrigation.

4. Caring for Sustainable Materials

Your eco-friendly materials, such as reclaimed wood, bamboo flooring, and natural fiber upholstery, require special care to keep them in excellent condition:

- **Reclaimed Wood:** Avoid using harsh chemicals when cleaning reclaimed wood furniture or flooring. Instead, opt for natural cleaning products like a vinegar and water solution. Regularly oil or seal wooden surfaces to maintain durability.
- **Bamboo Flooring:** Bamboo is durable but sensitive to excess moisture. Clean it with a damp (not wet) mop and use natural floor cleaners to prevent damage.

- **Non-Toxic Furniture:** If you've invested in VOC-free furniture and upholstery, keep it clean by vacuuming regularly and using eco-friendly fabric sprays.

5. Reducing Long-Term Waste

A sustainable home isn't just about initial choices—it's about reducing waste in the long run. Some ways to do this include:

- **Repair Instead of Replace:** If an energy-efficient appliance starts acting up, see if it can be repaired before replacing it. Many sustainable brands also offer extended warranties or repair programs.
- **Composting and Recycling:** Continue composting kitchen waste and recycling materials properly. Educating your household members on correct disposal methods can significantly reduce landfill contributions.
- **Mindful Consumption:** Avoid cluttering your home with unnecessary items that contribute to waste. Before making a new purchase, ask yourself whether it's essential and whether a more sustainable alternative exists.

Section 2: How to Continue Saving Energy and Water Daily

Sustainability is not just about making eco-friendly upgrades to your home—it's about incorporating small, daily habits that create a lasting impact. Even with energy-efficient appliances, solar panels, and low-flow water fixtures in place, the way you use them determines how much you truly save.

By adopting mindful behaviors in your everyday routine, you can maximize the benefits of your home's sustainable features while reducing your environmental footprint. In this section, we'll explore practical, easy-to-follow strategies for saving energy and water every day.

1. Energy-Saving Habits You Can Implement Right Away

Your home's energy consumption is largely determined by how efficiently you use your appliances, lighting, and heating or cooling systems. Here's how to keep your daily energy usage in check:

Use Appliances Wisely

Even the most energy-efficient appliances can be wasteful if not used properly. Simple changes in how you operate them can lead to significant savings.

- **Unplug Electronics When Not in Use** – Devices like TVs, coffee makers, and chargers continue to draw power even when turned off. Using a smart power strip or unplugging electronics when they're not in use can reduce "phantom energy" waste.
- **Run Full Loads in Dishwashers and Washing Machines** – A half-full dishwasher or washing machine uses the same amount of energy as a full one. Waiting until you have a full load before running these appliances maximizes efficiency.
- **Use Cold Water for Laundry** – Heating water accounts for a large portion of energy use in washing machines. Using cold water can significantly reduce energy consumption while also preserving fabrics.

- **Air Dry Clothes When Possible** – Instead of relying on a dryer, take advantage of natural air drying. This reduces electricity use and extends the life of your clothes.

Optimize Heating and Cooling

Heating and cooling account for the biggest chunk of household energy consumption. Smart adjustments can make a difference.

- **Adjust Thermostat Settings Wisely** – Set your thermostat a few degrees lower in winter and higher in summer. Each degree can save around 3% on your energy bill.
- **Use Curtains and Blinds to Your Advantage** – In winter, open curtains during the day to let sunlight warm your home and close them at night to retain heat. In summer, keep blinds closed during peak sun hours to prevent overheating.
- **Ceiling Fans Instead of Air Conditioning** – A ceiling fan uses far less energy than an AC unit. In warm weather, running a fan counterclockwise creates a cooling effect, while reversing it in winter helps distribute warm air.

Switch to Smarter Lighting

- **Use LED Bulbs** – LED bulbs use up to 80% less energy and last much longer than incandescent bulbs.
- **Turn Off Lights When Leaving a Room** – It sounds simple, but many people forget! Installing motion sensor lights can help automate this habit.
- **Maximize Natural Light** – During the day, use natural sunlight instead of artificial lighting whenever

possible. Position mirrors strategically to reflect light and brighten rooms.

---

2. Water-Saving Strategies for Everyday Living

Water is a precious resource, and even with water-efficient fixtures installed, the way you use water daily determines your overall savings. Here are effective ways to conserve water in the kitchen, bathroom, and beyond.

In the Bathroom

- **Turn Off the Tap While Brushing Teeth** – This small habit can save up to 8 gallons of water per day per person.
- **Take Shorter Showers** – Cutting shower time by just a couple of minutes can save thousands of gallons of water per year.
- **Install a Water-Saving Showerhead** – If you haven't already, low-flow showerheads can cut water usage by 50% without sacrificing pressure.

In the Kitchen

- **Use a Bowl for Rinsing Fruits and Vegetables** – Instead of running water continuously, fill a bowl to wash produce and then reuse the water for plants.
- **Avoid Using Running Water to Defrost Food** – Plan ahead and let frozen foods thaw in the refrigerator rather than under running water.
- **Scrape Plates Instead of Rinsing** – Wipe off excess food from dishes before loading them into the dishwasher to save water.

For Outdoor Water Use

- **Water Plants in the Morning or Evening** – This reduces evaporation and ensures plants absorb more water.
- **Use a Rain Barrel** – Collecting rainwater for gardening or outdoor cleaning can reduce your reliance on municipal water.
- **Choose Drought-Resistant Landscaping** – Native plants and xeriscaping require less water and maintenance.

---

3. Smart Tech to Help You Save Energy and Water

Technology can make it easier to track and reduce your energy and water usage. Here are some smart solutions that can help:

- **Smart Thermostats** – These learn your habits and adjust heating and cooling settings automatically, saving energy without compromising comfort.
- **Smart Water Meters** – Devices like Flo by Moen or Phyn detect leaks, track water usage, and provide real-time data on how much water you consume.
- **Energy Monitoring Plugs** – Smart plugs can help track energy usage of specific appliances and allow you to turn them off remotely.
- **Leak-Detection Sensors** – Placing sensors under sinks and near appliances can alert you to leaks before they become major problems.

4. Mindful Consumption: The Key to Long-Term Sustainability

Beyond adjusting habits and using technology, making conscious choices about what you buy and use daily plays a major role in conserving energy and water.

Reduce Single-Use Products

Opting for reusable alternatives cuts down on waste and manufacturing-related energy consumption.

- Replace disposable water bottles with stainless steel or glass bottles.
- Use cloth napkins instead of paper towels.
- Choose reusable shopping bags instead of plastic ones.

Invest in Quality Over Quantity

Buying well-made products that last longer prevents the cycle of constant replacements, reducing the energy and water used in manufacturing.

Embrace Minimalism in Your Home

The more items you own, the more resources are required to maintain them. Adopting a minimalist approach—focusing on essentials rather than excess—can help reduce waste and unnecessary consumption.

Final Thoughts: Small Steps, Big Impact

Saving energy and water daily is not about making drastic lifestyle changes overnight—it's about making small, consistent efforts that add up over time. By developing mindful habits, using technology to your advantage, and making conscious purchasing decisions, you can ensure that your home remains eco-friendly long after your renovations are complete.

As you continue your green journey, remember: sustainability is not a one-time project, but an ongoing commitment to living in harmony with the environment.

Section 3: Hosting an Eco-Friendly Household (Parties, Cleaning Routines, etc.)

A sustainable home isn't just about energy-efficient appliances and water-saving fixtures—it's about the choices you make every day. Hosting an eco-friendly household means adopting sustainable habits in every aspect of home life, from how you entertain guests to how you clean and maintain your space.

In this section, we'll explore practical ways to create a green home environment, whether you're throwing a party, establishing a sustainable cleaning routine, or making conscious choices in your everyday living.

1. Hosting Eco-Friendly Gatherings and Parties

Social events and family gatherings are a great way to celebrate and connect, but they can also generate a lot of waste and unnecessary consumption. With some thoughtful planning, you can throw an amazing event that's both enjoyable and environmentally responsible.

A Green Approach to Party Planning

When organizing a gathering, whether it's a birthday party, holiday dinner, or casual get-together, consider the following sustainability principles:

1. **Go Paperless with Invitations** – Instead of printed invitations, opt for digital ones via email, text, or event platforms like Evite or Paperless Post. This reduces paper waste while making it easy to track RSVPs.
2. **Encourage Guests to Carpool or Use Public Transport** – If guests are driving, encourage carpooling to reduce emissions. If feasible, offer biking or public transport suggestions.
3. **Host Outdoor or Daylight Events** – If possible, host gatherings during the day to take advantage of natural light, reducing electricity use. Outdoor spaces also require less air conditioning.

Sustainable Food and Drink Choices

The food and drinks served at gatherings often have a big environmental impact, from packaging waste to food miles. Here's how to make more eco-friendly choices:

- **Serve Local, Organic, and Seasonal Foods** – Locally sourced ingredients have a lower carbon footprint and often taste fresher.
- **Reduce Meat Consumption** – Offer more plant-based dishes, which are more sustainable than meat-heavy meals. If serving meat, opt for responsibly sourced, organic options.

- **Limit Single-Use Packaging** – Avoid individually wrapped snacks and drinks. Serve food in reusable dishes instead.
- **Use Reusable Dinnerware and Utensils** – Instead of disposable plates and cutlery, use real dishes or biodegradable alternatives like bamboo.
- **Provide a Water Station Instead of Bottled Water** – Set up a pitcher with filtered water and reusable glasses to avoid plastic waste.

Decorations and Party Supplies

Many party decorations are used once and then thrown away. Instead, try:

- **Reusable or DIY Decorations** – Fabric banners, LED string lights, and repurposed decorations can be used multiple times.
- **Compostable or Recycled Decorations** – If disposable items are needed, look for compostable tableware and recycled paper decorations.
- **Avoid Balloons and Glitter** – These contribute to microplastic pollution. Opt for flowers, potted plants, or handmade paper decorations instead.

Managing Waste After the Party

A responsible party host ensures minimal waste and proper disposal of leftovers.

- **Set Up Clearly Labeled Recycling and Compost Bins** – Help guests dispose of items properly.
- **Save and Share Leftovers** – Encourage guests to take home extra food in reusable containers, or donate edible leftovers to a local food bank.

- **Reuse Gift Wrap and Bags** – If gifts are exchanged, collect wrapping paper and gift bags for future use.

---

2. Creating a Sustainable Cleaning Routine

A green home should be cleaned in a way that supports both health and the environment. Many conventional cleaning products contain harsh chemicals that pollute indoor air and waterways. Adopting a more eco-friendly approach to cleaning can improve indoor air quality, protect the environment, and save money.

Choosing Green Cleaning Products

- **Use Natural Ingredients** – Many household cleaning tasks can be handled with vinegar, baking soda, lemon juice, and castile soap.
- **Avoid Harsh Chemicals** – Many commercial cleaners contain ammonia, chlorine, and synthetic fragrances, which can be harmful to health and the environment. Choose plant-based, biodegradable cleaners instead.
- **Make DIY Cleaning Solutions** – Instead of buying multiple cleaning products, make your own:
    - **All-Purpose Cleaner**: Mix equal parts water and vinegar with a few drops of essential oil.
    - **Glass Cleaner**: Combine 1 cup of water, 1 cup of vinegar, and 1 tablespoon of cornstarch.
    - **Natural Scrub**: Sprinkle baking soda on surfaces and scrub with a damp cloth.

Eco-Friendly Cleaning Tools

The tools you use to clean can also contribute to sustainability:

- **Opt for Reusable Cloths Instead of Paper Towels** – Microfiber cloths, rags, and sponges can be washed and reused.
- **Use Wooden Brushes and Natural Sponges** – Bamboo and coconut fiber brushes are durable and biodegradable.
- **Avoid Disposable Mop Pads and Swiffers** – Choose a mop with a washable head or a steam cleaner for floors.

Reducing Water and Energy in Cleaning

- **Sweep or Dry Mop First** – Reduce the need for wet mopping by removing dirt and dust beforehand.
- **Use Cold Water When Possible** – Hot water uses more energy; cold water works well for most cleaning tasks.
- **Air Dry Laundry and Cleaning Rags** – Instead of using a dryer, let items air dry on a rack or clothesline.

---

3. Everyday Sustainable Household Habits

An eco-friendly home is more than just energy-efficient upgrades; it's about consistent, mindful habits. Here are a few simple ways to maintain a green household:

Reduce Household Waste

- **Buy in Bulk** – This minimizes packaging waste and reduces trips to the store.
- **Choose Plastic-Free Packaging** – Opt for glass, metal, or compostable materials when buying products.

- **Compost Food Scraps** – Instead of throwing away vegetable peels and coffee grounds, compost them for use in your garden.

Save Energy in the Kitchen

- **Use the Right-Sized Burner for Pots** – This prevents wasted energy when cooking.
- **Cover Pots While Cooking** – Traps heat and speeds up cooking time.
- **Let Hot Food Cool Before Refrigerating** – Reduces the workload of your fridge.

Eco-Friendly Laundry Habits

- **Wash Clothes in Cold Water** – Saves energy and keeps clothes looking new longer.
- **Use a Drying Rack Instead of a Dryer** – Reduces energy consumption and extends fabric life.
- **Only Run Full Loads** – Saves both water and electricity.

Final Thoughts: Small Changes Make a Big Impact

Hosting an eco-friendly household doesn't mean sacrificing comfort or convenience—it simply means making smarter, more sustainable choices. Whether you're throwing a zero-waste party, adopting a natural cleaning routine, or reducing your home's energy footprint, every small effort adds up over time.

By incorporating these green habits into your daily routine, you're not only reducing waste and conserving resources, but also setting an example for others to follow. A sustainable lifestyle is a journey, not a destination, and every step you take brings you closer to a cleaner, healthier home.

Section 4: Teaching Kids About Sustainability

One of the most impactful ways to ensure a greener future is to educate the next generation about sustainability. Children are naturally curious and eager to learn, making them perfect candidates for adopting eco-friendly habits early in life. Teaching kids about sustainability doesn't have to be a dry, lecture-style experience—it can be fun, engaging, and something the whole family enjoys together.

This section explores practical, age-appropriate ways to teach kids about sustainability, helping them understand their role in protecting the planet while making green living a natural part of their daily routine.

---

1. Leading by Example: The Power of Parental Influence

Children learn best by watching what their parents do. If they see you practicing sustainability, they're more likely to adopt those habits themselves.

Making Sustainability a Normal Part of Family Life

- **Use Reusable Bags and Containers** – Let kids see you bring your own shopping bags and use reusable water bottles instead of plastic.
- **Be Conscious of Energy Use** – Involve kids in turning off lights, unplugging devices, and setting the thermostat to energy-efficient levels.

- **Reduce Food Waste** – Show them how to store leftovers properly and encourage them to finish their meals to minimize waste.
- **Make Secondhand Shopping Fun** – Instead of always buying new, take kids to thrift stores or swap items with friends.

Encouraging Conversations About the Environment

- **Talk About Why Sustainability Matters** – Use real-world examples like deforestation, climate change, or ocean pollution to help kids understand why eco-friendly choices matter.
- **Ask Their Opinions** – Get their thoughts on how the family can be more sustainable. Kids often have creative ideas!
- **Make Connections to Everyday Life** – Explain how turning off the tap saves water or how recycling helps reduce landfill waste.

---

2. Making Sustainability Fun and Engaging for Kids

Children are more likely to embrace sustainability when it feels like an adventure rather than a chore. Turning green habits into games and interactive activities helps them learn while having fun.

Eco-Friendly Challenges and Games

- **Energy-Saving Contest** – Challenge kids to see who can remember to turn off the most lights and electronics when not in use.

- **Recycling Sorting Game** – Make sorting recyclables a game by letting kids compete to see who can sort correctly the fastest.
- **Litter Cleanup Treasure Hunt** – Take kids to a local park or beach and challenge them to collect litter. Offer small rewards for participation.
- **Water Conservation Challenge** – Set a family goal to reduce water usage and track progress. Celebrate milestones with a fun activity.

DIY Crafts and Upcycling Projects

- **Turn Old Clothes into New Creations** – Let kids cut up old t-shirts to make tote bags, headbands, or stuffed animals.
- **Repurpose Jars and Containers** – Use empty jars for craft storage, plant pots, or homemade candle holders.
- **Create Art from Recyclables** – Encourage kids to build sculptures or paintings using cardboard, bottle caps, and other recyclable materials.

---

3. Teaching Kids About Food Sustainability

Food choices have a significant impact on the environment, and kids can play an active role in making sustainable choices.

Growing a Garden Together

One of the best ways to teach kids about sustainability is through gardening. Watching plants grow from seeds helps them understand the importance of food sources.

- **Give Them Their Own Small Garden Bed** – Even if it's just a container on a balcony, letting kids grow their own plants makes them feel responsible and engaged.
- **Teach About Composting** – Show kids how food scraps can be turned into nutrient-rich soil for the garden.
- **Let Them Pick What to Grow** – Kids are more likely to eat vegetables if they helped grow them. Allow them to choose fun plants like cherry tomatoes, strawberries, or herbs.

Reducing Food Waste at Home

- **Teach Portion Awareness** – Serve smaller portions and let kids ask for more if they're still hungry.
- **Get Creative with Leftovers** – Show kids how leftovers can be transformed into new meals.
- **Make "Use-It-Up" Meals** – Have a weekly meal where the family works together to use up food before it spoils.

---

4. Teaching Kids About Energy and Water Conservation

Helping kids understand the importance of conserving energy and water can make a huge impact on household sustainability.

Energy-Saving Tips for Kids

- **Unplug Electronics When Not in Use** – Teach kids that even when devices are off, they can still use power if left plugged in.

- **Use Natural Light** – Encourage them to open curtains during the day instead of turning on lights.
- **Limit Screen Time** – Less time on screens means less energy usage—and more time for outdoor play!

Water Conservation Lessons

- **Turn Off the Tap While Brushing Teeth** – A simple habit that can save gallons of water each week.
- **Use a Timer for Showers** – Make it a game to see who can take the shortest (but still effective) shower.
- **Collect Rainwater** – Teach kids how to collect and use rainwater for plants.

---

5. Introducing Kids to Nature and Wildlife Conservation

Kids who spend time in nature develop a deeper appreciation for the environment and are more likely to care for it.

Outdoor Adventures

- **Go on Nature Walks** – Take family hikes and discuss the plants, animals, and ecosystems you see.
- **Visit Farms and Wildlife Centers** – Let kids learn about sustainable farming and animal conservation firsthand.
- **Start a Birdwatching Journal** – Help kids identify local birds and track which ones visit your yard.

Helping Wildlife at Home

- **Create a Bee-Friendly Garden** – Plant flowers that attract bees and butterflies.

- **Build a Bird Feeder** – Teach kids how to make simple bird feeders using recycled materials.
- **Make a Wildlife Habitat** – Set up a small space in your yard with rocks, logs, and plants to attract insects and small creatures.

Final Thoughts: Raising the Next Generation of Eco-Conscious Citizens

Teaching kids about sustainability isn't about perfection—it's about making small, meaningful changes that add up over time. When kids grow up understanding the importance of reducing waste, conserving resources, and protecting nature, they carry those values into adulthood.

By making sustainability fun, interactive, and a natural part of everyday life, you're not just creating a greener home—you're shaping a future generation that cares for the planet.

Section 5: Inspiring Others – Sharing Your Green Home Journey

Creating a sustainable home is a powerful step toward protecting the environment, but the impact doesn't have to stop at your front door. By sharing your green home journey with others, you can inspire friends, family, and even your community to adopt more eco-friendly practices. Sustainability thrives when people support and learn from each other, making small changes that collectively lead to a significant positive impact.

This section explores how you can effectively share your journey, encourage others to embrace green living, and build a network of eco-conscious individuals who work together to create a healthier planet.

---

1. Leading by Example: The Power of Everyday Actions

The most effective way to inspire others is by living out your values. When people see the positive impact of your sustainable lifestyle, they're more likely to follow suit.

Being a Role Model

- **Demonstrate Sustainable Habits** – Use reusable bags, compost food scraps, and choose energy-efficient appliances. When others notice these habits, they may become curious and ask about them.
- **Show That Sustainability is Achievable** – People may assume an eco-friendly lifestyle is expensive or inconvenient. Show them that simple, cost-effective changes—like reducing food waste or using less water—can make a big difference.
- **Make It a Lifestyle, Not a Lecture** – Instead of telling people what they should do, let them see the benefits of sustainability in your own life.

Welcoming Questions and Discussions

- **Share Your Experiences Openly** – Talk about both the successes and challenges you've faced in making your home greener. This honesty makes sustainability more relatable and less intimidating.
- **Encourage Curiosity** – If someone asks about your compost bin or rainwater collection system, offer to explain how it works and why you use it.

2. Using Social Media to Spread Awareness

In today's digital world, social media is a powerful tool for sharing ideas and inspiring change. You don't have to be an influencer to make a difference—simple, personal posts can have a ripple effect.

Sharing Your Green Journey Online

- **Post Before-and-After Photos** – Show how your home has changed through sustainable renovations, gardening projects, or zero-waste swaps.
- **Write About Your Experiences** – Share what you've learned, the mistakes you've made, and tips for others who want to start their own sustainability journey.
- **Use Hashtags and Eco-Friendly Communities** – Platforms like Instagram, Facebook, and Twitter have thriving sustainability communities. Using hashtags like #SustainableLiving, #EcoFriendlyHome, or #GreenLiving can help your posts reach a wider audience.
- **Celebrate Small Wins** – Did you reduce your electricity bill by making energy-efficient upgrades? Save gallons of water by switching to drought-resistant landscaping? Share these successes!

Starting Conversations and Challenges

- **Eco-Friendly Challenges** – Encourage your followers to participate in fun sustainability challenges, like a "Plastic-Free Week" or a "Meatless Monday."
- **Ask Questions** – Post discussion prompts like "What's one small eco-friendly habit you've adopted?" to get people thinking and sharing their own experiences.

3. Hosting Green Gatherings and Community Events

Sometimes, the best way to spread sustainability is through direct engagement. Hosting eco-friendly events, workshops, or gatherings can be a fun and interactive way to bring people together.

Organizing Sustainable Home Tours

If you've made significant green upgrades to your home, consider opening your doors for a sustainability home tour. Invite friends, neighbors, or even local organizations to see your energy-efficient appliances, water-saving fixtures, or composting setup in action.

- **Keep It Interactive** – Let visitors try out features like your solar-powered irrigation system or see how your compost bin works.
- **Provide Takeaway Tips** – Create a simple handout with eco-friendly tips or a list of your favorite sustainable brands.
- **Make It Casual and Fun** – Offer refreshments made from locally sourced ingredients or organize a small giveaway with eco-friendly prizes.

Hosting Green-Themed Gatherings

- **Zero-Waste Dinner Parties** – Challenge guests to bring homemade dishes in reusable containers, and serve food with compostable or reusable dinnerware.
- **Eco-Friendly Craft Nights** – Teach friends how to make upcycled crafts, like turning old t-shirts into reusable bags or making homemade cleaning products.

- **Sustainability Workshops** – If you've mastered composting, gardening, or energy-efficient cooking, host a mini-workshop to share your knowledge.

---

4. Getting Involved in Local Sustainability Efforts

Community involvement is a fantastic way to amplify your impact. Many cities have local sustainability initiatives, and participating in them can help spread awareness while making tangible improvements in your area.

Joining or Starting Local Environmental Groups

- **Volunteer for Green Organizations** – Find local groups that focus on tree planting, recycling programs, or community gardens.
- **Advocate for Green Policies** – Attend city council meetings to support eco-friendly initiatives like improved recycling services or bike-friendly infrastructure.
- **Create a Community Swap or Repair Event** – Organize a local event where people can exchange items they no longer need or get help repairing broken items instead of throwing them away.

Encouraging Schools and Businesses to Go Green

- **Work with Schools** – Offer to give a short talk about sustainability or help implement a school recycling or gardening program.
- **Engage Local Businesses** – Support businesses that prioritize sustainability and encourage others to adopt greener practices, like offering refill stations for personal care products.

5. Building a Supportive Eco-Community

Creating a more sustainable world isn't a solo effort—it thrives when people work together. Surrounding yourself with like-minded individuals helps keep you motivated and inspires ongoing growth.

Finding Your Eco-Friendly Tribe

- **Connect with Other Green-Minded Individuals** – Join sustainability-focused Facebook groups, attend eco-friendly events, or participate in online forums.
- **Support and Uplift Each Other** – Share resources, success stories, and advice to encourage others on their journey.

Staying Inspired and Continuing to Learn

- **Keep Expanding Your Knowledge** – Follow sustainability blogs, read books, and watch documentaries to stay informed about new green practices.
- **Celebrate Progress, Not Perfection** – Encourage yourself and others to focus on progress rather than feeling guilty about not being perfectly sustainable.

Chapter 10 Summary: Embracing a Sustainable Lifestyle for the Long Term

Living sustainably doesn't end after renovating your home—it's an ongoing journey that involves maintaining eco-friendly habits, conserving energy and water, hosting a greener household, teaching kids about sustainability, and inspiring others to do the same.

This chapter explored:

- **Maintaining Your Sustainable Upgrades** – Keeping up with energy-efficient appliances, water-saving fixtures, and eco-friendly materials to ensure long-term sustainability.
- **Daily Energy and Water Conservation** – Simple habits like turning off unused lights, limiting water waste, and choosing renewable energy sources can have a lasting impact.
- **Hosting an Eco-Friendly Household** – Making green choices in household cleaning, party planning, and daily routines creates a healthier home for your family.
- **Teaching Kids About Sustainability** – Instilling green habits in children through fun activities, gardening, conservation challenges, and leading by example.
- **Inspiring Others to Live Sustainably** – Sharing your green home journey with family, friends, and the community, using social media, hosting eco-friendly events, and participating in local sustainability efforts.

Sustainability is not about being perfect; it's about making continuous, mindful choices that help create a better world. By maintaining your green lifestyle, teaching future generations, and spreading awareness, you're not only benefiting your own household but also helping build a more sustainable future for everyone.

Conclusion: Your Home, Your Impact

Celebrating Your Progress: Every Step Counts!

As you reach the end of this journey toward a more sustainable home and lifestyle, it's time to take a step back and truly celebrate how far you've come. Transforming your home into a greener, more eco-friendly space is not just about reducing energy consumption or cutting down on waste—it's about creating a meaningful impact on your life, your community, and the planet.

Every step you've taken, whether big or small, has contributed to something greater than yourself. Perhaps you started with minor changes, like switching to LED bulbs, reducing plastic use, or composting kitchen scraps. Or maybe you committed to larger renovations, such as installing solar panels, upgrading to energy-efficient appliances, or designing a drought-resistant landscape. No matter where you started or how much progress you've made, **each decision has brought you closer to a more sustainable way of living**.

Acknowledging the Wins—Big and Small

Often, when working toward a big goal, it's easy to overlook the small victories. But those small changes are what build lasting habits and long-term impact. Here are some wins worth celebrating:

- **Lower Utility Bills:** If you've noticed a decrease in your electricity or water bills, that's a tangible sign that your sustainable upgrades are working.
- **Less Waste, More Awareness:** If you're throwing away less food, composting more, or relying less on single-use plastics, you've successfully integrated waste reduction into your daily life.

- **A Healthier Living Space:** By choosing non-toxic cleaning products, improving indoor air quality, and incorporating natural materials, you've created a healthier home for yourself and your family.
- **Teaching and Inspiring Others:** If friends, family members, or neighbors have started making greener choices because of your influence, your impact is extending beyond your household.

Change is a process, and celebrating each milestone keeps you motivated. Rather than feeling overwhelmed by what's left to do, take a moment to appreciate how much you've already accomplished.

Reflecting on Your Sustainability Journey

Think back to the beginning of your journey. What inspired you to make these changes? What obstacles did you face, and how did you overcome them? **Every challenge you tackled has helped shape the sustainable home and lifestyle you now enjoy.**

- **Mindset Shifts:** Have you noticed yourself thinking differently about consumption, waste, or resource use? A sustainable mindset is one of the most powerful changes you can experience.
- **Improved Habits:** Maybe you now instinctively turn off unused lights, opt for reusable shopping bags, or prefer locally sourced foods. These small choices become second nature over time.
- **Financial Benefits:** Sustainability isn't just about the environment—it can also save money in the long run. Energy-efficient homes often have lower maintenance costs, and many sustainable practices (such as growing your own food) lead to financial savings.

Your progress is worth acknowledging because every effort contributes to a much larger movement toward a more sustainable future.

How Small Changes Create a Ripple Effect

You might wonder: **Can my personal efforts really make a difference?** The answer is a resounding yes. Small changes, when multiplied across communities and generations, create powerful ripple effects.

1. Leading by Example

When you embrace sustainability, people around you take notice. Your choices—whether it's refusing plastic straws, driving an electric vehicle, or growing your own herbs—can spark conversations and inspire others to rethink their habits.

Ways Your Actions Influence Others:

- **Friends and Family:** If they see you using reusable water bottles or reducing food waste, they may be encouraged to do the same.
- **Neighbors and Community:** Participating in local clean-ups, composting, or using solar energy can normalize sustainable practices in your area.
- **Future Generations:** Children, in particular, learn by observing. Your green habits can instill lifelong sustainable values in them.

2. The Social and Environmental Chain Reaction

Your actions don't just stay within your household. Every eco-friendly decision contributes to broader change:

- **Businesses Respond to Consumer Demand:** If more people choose eco-friendly products, companies adapt by offering more sustainable options.
- **Government Policies Shift:** Increased demand for renewable energy, waste reduction, and sustainable development can influence policies and infrastructure improvements.
- **Communities Evolve:** When more people embrace sustainability, local markets, schools, and institutions begin prioritizing green initiatives.

By taking small, consistent steps, you become part of a movement that extends far beyond your home.

Resources for Continued Learning and Sustainable Living

Sustainability is a lifelong journey. Staying informed and engaged ensures that you continue making progress and adapting to new innovations. Here are some valuable resources to help you keep growing on this path:

1. Books and Documentaries

Expand your knowledge with insightful documentaries:

- **Documentaries:**
    - *Our Planet* (Netflix)
    - *A Plastic Ocean* (Netflix)
    - *Minimalism: A Documentary About the Important Things* (Netflix)
    - *The True Cost* (focuses on sustainable fashion)

2. Websites and Online Communities

Engage with online platforms that provide tips, news, and discussions on sustainability:

- **Treehugger (www.treehugger.com)** – Covers everything from green architecture to zero-waste living.
- **Earth911 (www.earth911.com)** – Offers recycling guides and sustainability tips.
- **Permaculture News (www.permaculturenews.org)** – Focuses on regenerative farming and sustainable landscapes.

3. Apps for Sustainable Living

Technology can make sustainability more accessible:

- **Oroeco:** Tracks your carbon footprint and suggests ways to reduce it.
- **Good On You:** Rates fashion brands based on their ethical and environmental impact.
- **Too Good To Go:** Helps reduce food waste by connecting people with surplus food from restaurants and grocery stores.

4. Local and Community-Based Resources

Look for resources in your own community:

- **Farmers' Markets:** Support local agriculture and reduce your carbon footprint.
- **Composting Programs:** Many cities now offer composting services to reduce food waste.
- **Sustainability Workshops:** Community centers often host free or affordable classes on eco-friendly practices.

Encouragement to Keep Improving

No matter how much you've accomplished, there's always room for growth. Sustainability is not about perfection—it's about **consistent, mindful progress**.

1. Embracing Imperfection

You don't have to live a zero-waste lifestyle or install every green upgrade overnight. Focus on progress, not perfection. If you forget to bring your reusable bag or slip up on a sustainable habit, don't get discouraged—just keep moving forward.

2. Staying Inspired

Find new ways to challenge yourself:

- **Try a Month-Long Sustainability Challenge** – Reduce energy use, eat more plant-based meals, or limit single-use plastics.
- **Set Yearly Sustainability Goals** – Commit to one or two big improvements each year, such as installing solar panels or transitioning to an electric car.
- **Engage with Like-Minded People** – Stay motivated by connecting with others who share your passion for sustainability.

3. Your Home, Your Impact

Your green home is more than just a collection of eco-friendly upgrades—it's a reflection of your values, a commitment to the future, and a powerful example of how small changes lead to big results. Every step you take is a step toward a cleaner, healthier world. **So keep learning, keep growing, and keep inspiring those around you.**

About the Author

Jesintha is a passionate author dedicated to **sustainable living, creative expression, and mindful homemaking**. She writes **eco-friendly home renovation guides, coloring books for all ages (kids, adults, and seniors)**, **South Indian cookbooks, decluttering and home organization books, Christian parenting guides**, and **practical series on canning, preserving, and raised bed gardening**.

Her expertise in **sustainable home renovation** helps readers transform their living spaces with **energy-efficient upgrades, zero-waste solutions, and eco-conscious choices**. With a background in mathematics and engineering, she blends **logic with creativity** to provide **practical, easy-to-follow guides** for a greener and more organized home.

Whether you're looking to **renovate sustainably, embrace minimalism, grow your own food, or explore traditional cooking**, Jesintha's books empower you to create a **healthier, more sustainable lifestyle**.

Enjoyed the book? Share your thoughts! ⭐ ⭐ ⭐ ⭐ ⭐

Your feedback means the world! Leave a quick review and let others know how this book helped you.

Send your feedback to **Jesintha.Bhaskaran@gmail.com** – we'd love to hear from you!

Thank you for your support!

Made in United States
North Haven, CT
01 May 2025

68473519R00134